IMAGINEERING YOUR *Life* ®

7 PRINCIPLES *for* DESIGNING *and* BUILDING *an* EXTRAORDINARY LIFE

Siobhan McKenna

MORGAN JAMES PUBLISHING • NEW YORK

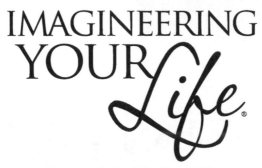

IMAGINEERING YOUR *Life*

For more information about Siobhan McKenna,
go to ImagineeringYourLife.com

ISBN: 978-1-61448-133-1 (Paperback)
   978-1-61448-134-8 (eBook)

Library of Congress Control Number: 2011937671

Published by:
MORGAN JAMES PUBLISHING
1225 Franklin Ave Ste 32
Garden City, NY 11530-1693
Toll Free 800-485-4943
www.MorganJamesPublishing.com

Cover/Interior Design: Rachel Lopez
 rachel@r2cdesign.com
Cover Concept: Harry F. Smith
 hfsmith@LikeADuckPublishing.com
Cover Photo: Kevin Connors
 kevin@CoastHighwayPhoto.com

In an effort to support local communities, raise awareness and funds, Morgan James Publishing donates one percent of all book sales for the life of each book to Habitat for Humanity. Get involved today, visit **www.HelpHabitatForHumanity.org.**

DEDICATION

This book is dedicated to my beautiful Mom and Dad
who always showed me such incredible love and encouragement.
I love and miss you both.
Every day.

TABLE OF CONTENTS

FOREWORD

I am a big fan of Siobhan McKenna. I love her energy, positive attitude, and enthusiasm for life. You will, too, if you read *Imagineering Your Life*. Who Siobhan is seems to jump off the pages into your heart. Why? Because she cares about you and me and wants us to have an extraordinary life like she has been able to design for herself.

Siobhan helping us design our lives is amazing considering her background. Her higher education includes studying mechanical engineering as well as earning Bachelor's degrees in the fields of architecture and computer science. For almost two decades, she has helped design and develop large, complex computer systems in the aerospace/defense industry.

To help people design and build extraordinary lives, Siobhan has not turned her back on her left brain computer science work. In fact, her efforts in life planning were inspired by an architectural framework for developing and building enterprise intelligent computer systems. As a result, she will help you answer these seven important questions—The What, the Why, the How, the Who, the Where, the When, and the Action - for designing a life filled with love, success, fun, adventure, wealth, and excellent health.

If you think that's not a bad deal for your life, read on. I guarantee you that *Imagineering Your Life,* with Siobhan as your guide, will be a journey well worth the time. Enjoy.

> **—Ken Blanchard**
> Coauthor of *The One Minute Manager*
> and *Lead with LUV*

INTRODUCTION

"We are what we repeatedly do.
Excellence then is not an act, but a habit."

—ARISTOTLE

I always thought how wonderful it would be if each of us had a tool belt filled with exactly what we needed to build an extraordinary life. A life filled with love, success, fun, adventure, wealth, and excellent health. There are so many facets to our lives that at times it can be overwhelming. As we move through life, we are often faced with difficult decisions, significant obstacles, and enormous challenges. I came to realize in my heart of hearts that there must be some type of formula or foundation available to help us create the life of our dreams.

The notion that individuals could be the architects of their own lives resonates deeply inside me. After all, we build our life every day, consciously or unconsciously. When looked at like this, every decision you make is like another line on the drawing board of your life. You are literally "Imagineering Your Life." In thinking about our lives this way, we tend to be much more cognizant of the choices we make, the people we choose to be with, and the environments in which we live, work, and play.

Following the paradigm of asking great questions to get great answers, I returned to the fundamental questions we ask about any subject: who, what, where, when, and how. Through meticulously working to create a clear vision of your future life, you are taking the first steps towards reaching your goals and living a more successful and accomplished life. The goal of leading an extraordinary life is to create a clear vision of one's life. By envisioning one's life, we will be able to lay a strong foundation for the lives we were all meant to have.

Think about it this way, without a strong foundation and solid understructure, a building would fall over and collapse. Likewise, when correlating this concept to our lives, it is essential to establish a plan and a strong foundation to achieve that life plan.

We can get so caught in life that, by the time we stop and look around, life has happened to us and slipped through our hands like the sands of time. To truly live life to its fullest, you have to grasp it, nurture it, and be the star of it, rather than having an occasional cameo. We all need to be proactive versus reactive when creating the circumstances of our lives; thus our life's foundation needs to be truly thought out and prepared for. Most people spend more time planning their summer vacation than they do designing their lives. Wouldn't it be nice if we had a literal "life tool belt" to help build unlimited success in every area of our lives?

If it is possible to design and develop billion dollar complex computer systems and build architectural masterpieces, then why isn't it possible to use those same principles for designing and building an extraordinary life?

Just for a second, I want you to imagine that you are an architect. While you normally build big, beautiful homes for others, today is your day. You have finally decided to build your dream home, to architect the perfect place to spend your life, the one that has always been in your dreams. While you have a vision firmly planted in your mind, you need to design the plans. Only when all of the steps have been finalized and committed to paper will it be time to build. After the blueprint has been created, you will be ready for construction.

I modeled the concepts in this book from real-world architectural frameworks that are currently used in the computer industry. Numerous frameworks are used to build engineering solutions, and the one that inspired the idea for *"Imagineering Your Life"* is known as the Zachman Architectural Framework.

This architectural framework used for designing and building intelligent enterprise computer systems provides a structured way of viewing and defining an enterprise. Enterprise systems recognize the need for providing accurate, consistent and timely information. Basically, the concept of creating enterprise intelligent systems ensures the availability of critical business information throughout the development of whatever you are designing and building. The same correlates to your life. You are the enterprise.

The framework consists of a two-dimensional classification matrix based on the intersection of six communication questions why, what, who, how, where, and when, that I mentioned earlier. You do not need to be an engineering expert to utilize this conceptual engineering tool to help build your life. We will use this same concept and framework in designing your life plan in this book.

When trying to build a successful life, you have to understand the make-up of your life. Imagine your life as a big pie, broken down into seven different pieces. Each slice carries a very specific value and purpose to your livelihood. Take one away and your pie is incomplete. You want to ensure you have this pie divided evenly into these seven pieces, so they each receive the right amount of attention and your life remains balanced.

As we move through this book, we will embark on a journey together through these seven fundamental principles for architecting and Imagineering a fantastic life. You have the power to build the life that you have dreamed of. And these principles will not only help you to dream of this life, but also to make it a reality.

The Principles

This book is divided into seven chapters, each presenting a relatable and useful tool that with a little bit of work and dedication, you can implement into your daily routine and move closer to Imagineering your ideal life.

> 1st PRINCIPLE: **The Inspiration**

What Makes Your Heart Soar

Why are you here? What inspires you? What do you absolutely love to do?

> 2nd PRINCIPLE: **The Vision**

Imagineering Your Own Life

What is your vision for your ultimate life? What end results do you ultimately want?

> 3rd PRINCIPLE: **The Blueprint**

Laying the Foundation

How are you going to design your master life plan?

> 4th PRINCIPLE: **The Architect**

You Are the Master Builder

You are the person responsible for creating this extraordinary life. How do your routines and daily life habits support your vision?

> ➤ 5th PRINCIPLE: **The Site**

Eye on Paradise

Where is this magnificent life going to happen?

> ➤ 6th PRINCIPLE: **The Timeline**

Just Now

When is this life going to begin? What are the major milestones for you to begin to plan it out?

> ➤ 7th PRINCIPLE: **The Action**

Now, Go Build It

Without action, all bets are off. What actions are you going to take to achieve what you have set out to achieve?

You will receive the benefit of some basic and fun tools for building and creating your extraordinary life from reading this book. You will also read stories that will enlighten and entertain while you stock your tool belt. Finally, you will learn the basic building blocks needed to get you moving and on your way.

I am passionate about helping people. I want to help people, and sometimes you just need special tools in your tool belt to help answer, "How do I create that ultimate life? How will it look for me?"

It is helpful to ask good questions in order to get your juices flowing and ask yourself, "What do I really want?" I have gone through this process many times trying to identify what inspires me. To help you through this process, I have created questions at the end of each chapter that will help you to figure out certain aspects of your life. I call these questions "Plus Up" and once you reach the end of the first chapter, you will understand exactly why. If you are serious about wanting to re-design your life, take the time to answer these questions thoughtfully and thoroughly. The questions will help provide insight and allow you the opportunity to reflect on not only where you stand in your current life, but also where you want to be as time goes on.

As each chapter closes, you will also find what I call "Snippets." These "Snippets" are short but powerful examples of the power of engineering in the real world. Each one has a theme and relates to the preceding chapters and demonstrates the fantastic ability to inspire, build, architect, dream, and act.

I believe in you and want to see you shine. May this launching of your true life's journey, passion, and purpose be filled with true accomplishment, achievement and happiness. The world is just a great big sandbox for us to play in, build our castles, and leave our marks.

So, strap on that tool belt <u>and</u> roll up your sleeves; it's time to get moving.

1

The Inspiration

WHAT MAKES YOUR HEART SOAR?

"The truth of knowing which risks to take is after taking them; does your heart dance and your spirit soar? If not, let them go and find ones that do."

—DAVID D. DAVIDSON (MY DAD)

Inspiration

What truly inspires people? What is it that makes one person rise to the heights of success while another is fulfilled and happy making a smaller life for oneself? It all comes down to that one question - what makes your heart soar? What is the one thing you absolutely love to do? What is that thing, that activity, that when you are doing it you are so incredibly in the moment, right in the here and now? In life, there are things that resonate, that reverberate in each of us. It could be your family, your friends, your job, your charity, and anything and everything in between.

These are the things that clutch onto our heart and inspire us to move, to wake up, to put one foot in front of the other, and to live a meaningful and successful life. We all have these stimulating and motivating pieces to our life. And before you can even start to imagineer your ideal life, you have to have a basic understanding of what moves you to go farther, work harder, and never give up until you reach your goals.

Look deep inside yourself and begin to think about exactly what inspires you. When you wake up in the morning, what do you look forward to each and every day? Ever have one of those times in your life? Think back to a time when you were the happiest. What were you doing? Where were you? Who were you with? Imagine if you could do what you love every day of your life. Think about how happy you would be if you woke up each morning and did not have to snooze, or delay, or take your time to start your day. You rushed, even ran, to get your day moving. And the reason why? The answer is because you were inspired and motivated in your life.

I once saw an older man delivering flowers in my neighborhood; I said to him, "You must love your job. Everybody loves to get flowers and they are so happy to see you at their door." He said, "I was an engineer for thirty-three years. I retired and this is the happiest I have ever been in my life. I work two to three days a week, and people always smile and are so happy to see me. It is a wonderful life."

Wow, I thought to myself. "How cool that must be." This man lives a life that inspires him. To some, delivering flowers may not be as fulfilling and challenging as being an engineer, but to this one man, it was one job that truly mattered. The same can be true in your life. Your inspiration does not have to resonate with every individual in this world, only you.

If an activity makes you happy, and keeps you warm inside, that is what you should be doing. Begin asking yourself how you can live an inspired life and begin taking the steps to making that dream become a reality.

Here are a few examples of well-known people doing what they love to do and making a wonderful living at it.

➢ Oprah Winfrey, Ellen DeGeneres - Talking

➢ Sandra Bullock, Meryl Streep - Acting

➢ Lance Armstrong - Biking

➢ Faith Hill, Celine Dion - Singing

➢ Barbara DeAngelis, Jack Canfield - Speaking/Writing

These are some famous examples, but there are thousands upon thousands of ordinary people out there doing extraordinary things; those things that they absolutely love to do. And that is part of the reason why they are so good at it. When you do something that you love, you will always give 100% of your effort and heart into it. And it will show. It is crystal clear the Oprah's of the world absolutely adore waking up and going to work. It shows in their attitude, their ability, and ultimately, their success.

Every Day Counts

Every day presents an opportunity to be inspired. Many times, you may wake up in the morning and simply want to lie in bed. That is all fine and dandy every now and again, but inspiration comes in strange packaging, and only when you dive headfirst into all that the world has to offer will you have inspiring experiences. Each and every day on this earth is an occasion to find the fire that drives your soul and fuels your journey. And every day that you choose not to open your mind and your eyes to the potential for inspiration is, in my view, an unfulfilled day.

Imagine jumping out of bed every day in complete anticipation of the day ahead, a life where you are completely in the moment filled with happiness and peace. What is that place for you? What inspires you? What makes your heart and spirit soar? Make each day extraordinary. This simple statement is completely profound. When we look at life, all we truly have is each day. Today is that day. Each moment is precious. Each moment is new. Embrace the chance to drink life in.

I can remember one day when I had the choice to either stay at home or to venture out to see Lance Armstrong compete in a bike race a mile away. I look back at these words and wonder why there was ever a question. I did go see him race and am so happy I made that choice. I was truly inspired watching this amazing athlete. He won that day and I was there, front and center, to watch this inspirational man who survived cancer perform at an unbelievable level. It was so clear that he was in a league of his own. To think that I almost did not go watch the world's number one cyclist race by in my own town.

If I did not go, I would have heard about the amazing experience from my friends for weeks to come, and carried around regret for missing this opportunity. But instead, I can look back and be the one telling the inspirational story. The same should be true in your life. Do not miss out on great experiences because you are too tired, or ambivalent, or just not in the mood, because life will offer these inspirational moments to someone, so why not make sure it is you?

Clapping Among Strangers

Inspiration can come in all shapes and sizes. Often times, the purest type of inspiration comes in the form of something that we see with our own two eyes. These beautiful visions can move you to emotion and rouse up some of the most wholesome and warm feelings. For example, I frequently look to mother nature for some of the most surreal and magnificent examples of how truly amazing life can be. These inspirational moments are not only free, but also powerful and overwhelming.

I remember the first time I watched a sunset at the beach in San Diego. People huddled together on blankets, others on the sea wall, and some enjoyed glasses of champagne in their hands. It was almost as if a big event was about to happen. People on their bicycles stopped riding for a moment and leaned up against the wall. Rollerbladers were also taking a break.

I remember looking around in awe, at all the smiling faces with an inner knowing that an extraordinary event was about to happen -- like a crack in the air. All heads suddenly turned towards the sun as it began to sink into the beautiful blue ocean. A silence fell among the gathered anticipating crowd when just then the incredible colors emanating from this big ball of fire streaked across the sky.

I have experienced many sunsets, but this one seemed almost magical. To my amazement and delight, when the sun had completely fallen away, everyone started to clap. It was an absolutely wonderful feeling of pure joy. All of us who shared in this experience were inspired and motivated. We all felt profound and unfathomable warmth in our hearts.

When I feel uninspired, I can reminisce about that moment in time and it stirs up a little fire in my belly. Sharing the experience with these complete strangers was incredible. I joined in with a big smile on my face, and my heart filled with the celebration of yet another beautiful day here on this magnificent planet Earth.

But it does not stop with nature. Inspiration is everywhere. The Taj Mahal for instance, is a beautiful architectural wonder. Built by the Emperor Shah Jahan, in memory of his third wife, Mumtaz Mahal. It stands as a symbol of eternal love. How much love and emotion the emperor must have felt for his wife; I find that kind of devotion awe-inspiring. Some other inspiring architectural phenomena are things like the Egyptian pyramids, built for the pharaohs, because they believed when they died, they became immortal. They are simply breathtaking for so many reasons.

Have you ever seen the National Cathedral in Washington, D.C.? It is a cathedral of the Episcopal Church and also the sixth-largest cathedral in the entire world. It is an absolute work of art. Hundreds of people worked on the cathedral over an eighty-three-year period of time begun in 1907. Work continued through two world wars, the Great Depression and a shortage of funds. Yet despite these setbacks and delays, the dreamers and believers progressed forward and trusted that their dream would come true.

> *"I love this work. I can't envision getting up*
> *in the morning and not going to build a cathedral."*
>
> —A CATHEDRAL WORKER

These amazing architectural feats are everywhere. From the Golden Gate Bridge, to the Great Wall of China, to the Vatican, or Michelangelo's David, in this life, inspiration lies in every corner of the world.

Magnificence is all around us in complete silence. Take a moment each day to appreciate and be grateful for these natural amazements and these architectural triumphs, because they will push you, motivate you, and inspire you to do great things in your own life.

> *"All our dreams can come true,*
> *if we have the courage to pursue them."*
>
> —WALT DISNEY

Dream Big Dreams

We have spent a great deal of time speaking about the importance of finding inspiration. Whether it be from Mother Nature, an amazing piece of architecture, or one of the great wonders of the world, a life without inspiration is a life without color. But once you find your inspiration, what do you do with it? Well to begin with, inspiration is a catalyst for your dreams. When you are inspired, your mind is set free and you can dream for the future, and begin to imagineer your ideal life.

Not so long ago, I remember asking a fellow engineer who had worked in the aerospace industry for over forty years the following question, "What are your dreams?"

He replied, "What do you mean?"

I repeated the question, "What do you dream about?"

After a minute's thought, he declared, "I don't understand what you mean."

I was absolutely floored. I responded, "Wow, I thought everyone dreamed big dreams."

I believe that it is important to have dreams no matter what your age is because you can obtain whatever you want, but first you have to dream it. Dreams are the mechanism that allow us to visualize our future. More than anything, they are the destination for our journey. And it is only natural to dream big. And why not? It does not take more time or cost more money to dream big. There is no downside to big, beautiful, aspirations. Setting considerable goals and extensive dreams is what will keep you moving through life. And even if you do not reach your dreams, if you come close, it will have been a worthwhile journey.

Let's take a minute now and focus on your dreams. Name and identify something that you enjoy doing so much that you find it all encompassing and the world just seems to fall away when you are doing it. That is what we call your passion. Take your passion and your inspiration and let those drive that big diesel engine powering your dreams. Once you do that, you will be well positioned to create great expectations for you and your future life.

Searching for Golf Balls

When it comes to dreaming big, it is vital to dream like a child. Remember when you were a child and always dreamed of being a professional athlete, singer, or entertainer? As difficult as it is to break into these industries, when you are a child, you do not think of these formalities. You just dream and do it on a big level. Today, as adults, we often forget how to dream big and be inspired at an amazingly high level.

I once played a game with my ten-year-old nephew Dylan one night when he was over at my home. I asked him, "Dylan, what do you dream of being?"

He answered, "I'm going to be an NFL kicker."

I said, "That's wonderful, you'll make the best kicker ever since you are great at kicking. I am very happy to hear that!"

Later on that day, while we were hunting for golf balls at my home on the golf course, I told Dylan, "When you are a famous NFL kicker, you can come hide out at Auntie's and we can search for golf balls so you can get away from all the paparazzi and take a break from the fame of it all." I then told him that it's important to dream and never let anyone tell you that you are crazy for thinking you can become anything you want to be.

Have you ever thought in that way? Life can catch us by surprise and before we know it, we are all grown-up adults. Sometimes it can be nice to reflect back to that pure childhood time of dreaming that anything is possible. I welcome you to take a few moments and reflect back on some of your happiest childhood memories. How carefree life was at times. Maybe in the tree house, after school where you shared all your twelve-year-old secrets with your very best friends, or sleepovers that you actually never went to sleep at-- Laughing so hard that the night went by in what felt like minutes.

Sometimes we just need to let go and be that kid again. Searching for golf balls doesn't need to end when we're all grown up. Think for a moment you are that kid. You can incorporate that soul back into your life, which by the way has never left. Which one characteristic from when you were a kid would you start to embrace if you had the choice once again?

Ponder for a Moment

Your Dreams. Inspiration and passion fuel your big dreams. They provide you the welcomed chance to really go for it with your future aspirations. If you pursue what your heart tells you, I know that your dreams will come true. You will be able to realize that dream of traveling to all of the Architectural wonders of the world, or getting a promotion, or building a family, or whatever you want to accomplish. You have the ability to do it!

So to help you begin your dreaming, consider answering the questions provided below. They will help you brainstorm and give you direction through your journey to big dreams and fulfilling those big dreams.

Answer the following questions for your extraordinary life. I have provided my personal responses to demonstrate how to approach these questions:

> *The Why? Why do I dream big?*

I am at peace, happy, and love my beautiful, peaceful life. By helping and making other people happy, I know I am fulfilling that goal.

> ➤ *The What? What do I dream about?*

I have fun, love, and happy relationships. Most of all I want to help others.

> ➤ *The How? How will I begin to reach my dreams?*

I am grateful every day, learn each day, read and set goals. Having mentors who have already done what I ultimately want to do in life to help me get to where I want to be much faster.

> ➤ *The Who? Who am I in my dreams?*

I am smart, successful, fun loving, and healthy. By making affirmations, I will be confident and comfortable in my own skin interacting with other like-minded people.

> ➤ *The Where? Where will I find inspiration for my dreams?*

I spend my time amongst beauty and nature. This gives me peace of mind and provides me a quiet place to share my knowledge and wisdom in the written word.

> ➤ *The When? When will I begin to implement my dreams?*

I move toward this ideal life each and every day. How? By setting goals and specific time lines for the things I want to do. Then, when I look back at my life, I want to be able to see what I've accomplished and the lives I have touched.

> ➤ *The Action? What will I do to become inspired to dream?*

What can I do to make this extraordinary life happen? I will write down my goals, and then take the necessary action steps. Identifying and taking each step, gets me closer to them.

Now write down your answers to the questions for envisioning your extraordinary life:

➢ *The Why?*

_____

_____

_____

➢ *The What?*

_____

_____

_____

➢ *The How?*

_____

_____

_____

➢ *The Who?*

_____

_____

_____

➢ *The Where?*

_____

_____

_____

➢ *The When?*

_____

_____

_____

➢ *The Action?*

_____

_____

_____

Once you finish this exercise, take these answers and put them in a safe place. This is the first of many exercises we will go through toward the end of each chapter. The purpose of this activity is to help you find your inspiration and then figure out how to turn your inspiration into a real life dream. As we progress through the upcoming chapters, we will work together to take these big aspirations and dreams and make them a reality.

Snippets

Following each chapter I have included a section titled "snippets." Snippets are examples of actual feats of engineering and architecture. Making room to enlighten, entertain, and embrace the light you bring to your own life and others into the world of human potential.

I share with you these examples because I am inspired by the will of human endeavor and achievement. We can create greatness in our lives but most importantly we deserve happiness and peace. My goal being after reading the "snippets" included at the end of each chapter, you feel some lightness in your heart, possibly believing anything is truly possible in your own life. If nothing else, they are just really cool facts. So please enjoy and for a moment escape into the world of imagination and possibilities.

Snippets: Inspiring Achievement

Golden Gate Bridge

The Golden Gate Bridge in San Francisco, California was completed in 1937. It was a magnificent site and had become the longest suspension bridge in the world. The bridge has a 4,200 ft (1,280 m) section without any supporting pillars, an inspirational achievement in engineering which had taken close to four years to build.

Channel Tunnel

The Channel Tunnel referred to as the Chunnel is a 31.4 mile (50 km) undersea rail tunnel. The tunnel links the UK to France and carries high-speed passenger trains. The project was thought about as early as 1802, but did not begin construction until 1988 when it successfully opened in 1994.

Sydney Harbor Bridge

The Bridge opened in 1932 and was one of the greatest engineering masterpieces of its time. The main span is 1,650 ft (503m) across. It consumed more than 52,800 tons of silicon based steel tresses. More than six million steel rivets hold these plates of steel together. From start to finish the bridge (nicknamed the Coathanger) took eight years to complete and now carries vehicular, rail, bicycle, and pedestrian traffic across its span.

Note to Reader: *I had the wonderful fortune to actually climb the Sydney Harbor Bridge. An amazing, unbelievable experience. I highly recommend it if you ever find yourself in the beautiful city of Sydney. (www.bridgeclimb.com)*

Plus Up

"Plus Up" means once your project or idea is complete, take one more look and see if you can make it just a little better. It is the phrase used by the Disney Imagineers (the division of the Walt Disney Company that designs, develops and creates all aspects of the Disney theme parks worldwide) when they are creating any of their many wonderful creations. The Imagineers ask questions to think of how to make "it" better. Whatever they are working on such as a new theme park ride, a new show, or anything that enhances the guest experience.

The reason that Disney's Imagineers "Plus Up" is because they are expected to settle for nothing but excellence to literally exceed the theme park guest's expectations. Good enough just isn't good enough for the Imagineers. In thinking about what you want, I want you to approach your own life in the same way. You deserve excellence. While it may not come to you right away, excellence is what you should seek. The list of questions below is my way of getting you to "Plus Up" your life.

Before we start, I want to give you a bit of background about how I came up with this exercise. When I first did a brainstorming session during an engineering class in college, I realized the best way to figure out what you actually want is to get your ideas out of your head and onto paper. This consists of breaking down what you want into individual manageable chunks of information and thoughts onto a blank piece of paper.

Start this brainstorming session with a piece of paper and a quiet place to think. Now set a timer for five minutes and answer the following questions with whatever comes to mind. You can skip around if you get stuck on one question. Don't put so much thought into what you are going to write.

This is just free form writing so just go for it.

> What makes your heart sing and soar? I want you to think of what would really enhance your life.

> What, when you are doing it, makes the world fall away, putting you just completely in the moment?

> Take a moment to reflect on a time in your life when you were most inspired. What was it? How does that make you feel?

> Do you know what inspires you? If so, what is it?

➤ What brings you the most peace?

➤ At what times in your life were you happiest?

➤ When in your current life are you happiest?

➤ What activates your senses and makes you feel alive?

➤ Inspiration means "in spirit." What is your inspiration for getting out of bed each day?

➤ What would be your ultimate day if making money was not an issue?

➤ If you could imagine where you would play all day in a sandbox building your version of castles in the sky, where would you be and what would that "sandbox" look like?

After you have finished this task, put the answers to these questions away for at least 24 hours. Then go back and read what you've written. Having answered these questions thoughtfully, you should be able to assess what you love to do and what inspires you towards greatness. Now that you've established what your inspirations and dreams are, let's build on these concepts to identify what your ideal life vision could be.

Throughout this chapter, we focused on the crucial role that inspiration plays in your ability to imagineer your perfect life. If you are inspired, anything is possible. Finding this inspiration can come in many different mediums. Nature, architecture, world-wonders, family, friends, loved ones, and anything and everything in between can be sources of personal inspiration. Once you find that inspiration, your goal will be to convert it into big dreams. While that may seem to be a challenging task at first, with the exercises presented above, you will almost certainly be able to look into your heart and figure out what your dreams may be. Once you do that, you are taking enormous steps to Imagineering your ideal future and meeting all of your goals and aspirations.

2
The Vision
IMAGINEERING YOUR OWN LIFE

*"Your imagination is your preview
of life's coming attractions."*

—ALBERT EINSTEIN

Create the Vision

I t still amazes me that so many people do not have a clear-cut vision of their ultimate lives. Many are completely resigned to the hand they have been dealt. Others feel that their success is just luck. Some people feel trapped in their lives and that they don't have choices or opportunities for change. If many of these people would only focus on the, "How can I" instead of the "I can't because," their lives would

17

quickly turn around for the better. It all comes down to your attitude, your perspective and your choice of how you want to live life.

In life, many people make excuses for their lives. There is always a reason why certain people could not accomplish something they claimed they wanted to do. For example, I knew that I wanted to go to college more than anything. While I could have made excuses for why it wasn't financially feasible, I figured out a way. Nothing was going to stop me and I decided very early in my life that I would make the necessary sacrifices to achieve this goal. I had a definitive vision and belief in my heart that I would succeed, so I found ways to make it happen.

Before you can implement your ideal vision, it is vital to create a detailed and specific game plan for your ultimate goals. It all starts with your inner purpose and deciding exactly what you are trying to achieve with your journey. Too many people use obstacles as excuses to derail their vision. It is vital to your growth and success to take all of the reasons why you cannot succeed and simply throw them in the garbage. Excuses are nothing more than crutches, and those crutches will only prevent you from reaching your goals.

You do have a choice. You always have a choice. There is always a way. Give it a shot next time you find yourself making an excuse or faltering. Step inside that strong person you know is deep inside you and choose to take the higher road. This chapter is focused on the 'what' part of your life. What is the vision for your life? What end result do you want? Finding the answers to these difficult questions will be the focus of the upcoming sections.

Vision is defined as "the ability to think about or plan the future with imagination or wisdom." We all have a fantastic imagination that is ready to be unlocked. The key to unlocking this vision is in our heart and our mind. During our journey through life, our experiences provide crucial insight and wisdom to project our imagination to the world. This chapter will focus on finding your essential vision and using your imagination to maximize its powerful potential. Creating a roadmap for your vision is the first step that every imagineer needs to take....

> *"The thing always happens that you really believe in, and the belief in a thing makes it happen.."*
>
> —FRANK LLOYD WRIGHT

Great Creators

There is a good reason for naming this chapter "The Vision - Imagineering Your Own Life." When you imagineer your own life, it all starts with having a vision into what you would like to accomplish. Without a vision and an imagination, often times you can lose your path and may have trouble focusing on your destination.

Walt Disney is a great example of a visionary who focused on his destination, while using his imagination like a lighthouse, guiding him in the direction he wished to go. Today, we may think of Walt Disney as just the name of a Fortune 500 Company, but in fact, Walt Disney himself was a true visionary. His artistic contributions changed our world. He not only created a legacy of storytelling excellence in his classic animated movies, but he also created the concept of family destination fun when he conceived the idea of Disneyland in Anaheim, California in the early 1950's.

Walt Disney realized that there wasn't a great amusement park to take his own children for a fun outing (most of the country's amusement parks in post-war America were fairly rundown enterprises). That was his personal vision. Walt and his team began to develop and design a theme park that would be the first of its kind, spearheaded by his colorful imagination of course. Walt's vision was to use his expertise in storytelling to create more than rides but to create theme park attractions that told stories and created adventures of their own. He wished to create a place that transported its visitors into another world.

To accomplish this overwhelmingly original concept, Walt assembled a team of engineers, architects, show designers, artists, writers, directors and many others. Originally, Walt dubbed this company as WED Enterprises (WED are his initials) which was later renamed *Disney Imagineering* to reflect the division's focus on the combination of imagination and science/engineering to create original never-been-seen-before guest experiences.

The mandate at Disney Imagineering was and is to think outside of the box. People oftentimes flippantly talk about thinking "outside of the box." Meaning, to remove all constraints of the why not's, the cannots, and the can't be dones from your thought process. Rarely do we ever think without these constraints. Part of what I want to impart to you in this book is how to free yourself to think this way—with a lightness and freeness in your mind.

Like the Imagineers, it is important to take advantage of the power of both your creative side (right brain thinking) and your rational side (left brain thinking). By banding together these different ways of thinking, using both sides of your brain, you can design a life plan that shoots for the moon and dares to be fearless. But it starts with shedding the handcuffs of restraint, the ones that prevent you from freethinking, visionary forethought, and an imagination that runs rampant with liberated thoughts.

Walt Disney was successful because he had a pinpoint and razor sharp vision. He knew his ultimate goal was to create an empire built on telling stories and fairytales. He wanted to bring fantasy to life in an array of happiness and escapism. That was his vision and it was fueled by his unfettered imagination. That is what he woke up for each and every day of his life. And that is what kept him focused. The same is true for

Imagineering your own life. You have to ask yourself "what is my vision"? Where do I want to go today? Your vision is like your navigation. It keeps you on track and moving in the direction in which you must travel to reach your destination.

"Shoot for the Moon.
Even if you miss you will land among the Stars"

—Anonymous

The Journey to Your Ideal Vision

The journey to your ideal vision comes in many different ways. Think of the great writers, artists, architects, and dreamers. What did they imagine and think about each day? From where did their inspiration derive? How did the greatest of the great move beyond conventional thinking to go for their dream vision of life? Each of these visionaries took a different journey to make their dreams a reality, but through and through, the vision was their motivation and the motivation was their vision.

The master builders of the National Cathedral, an architectural masterpiece located in Washington, D.C., dreamed about building a magnificent cathedral. That was their fundamental vision. Each day, they were happy envisioning and building the magnificent structure. Implementing their imagination and fulfilling their vision was a meaningful way to spend their days, which makes for an enriched, fulfilled, and happy life. As their journey became a reality, the payoff was magnificent. They were not only applauded for their work, but they had a phenomenal sense of purpose and happiness as they worked together to build this amazing architectural work.

The journey to your ideal vision is a fantastic opportunity to Imagineer an electric life, one resonating with energy and excitement. So many people forget that they are the captains of their voyage and it is their personal responsibility to ensure their journey is meaningful. Engineers work day in and day out to build intricate and detailed systems that change the world. It is their job to create a path for the implementation of a successful product, whatever it may be.

Since we can engineer systems at such a complex and integrated level, why can't we do that with our lives? We all have the opportunity to Imagineer a wonderful life, one that fulfills not only our needs, but also all of our dreams. And it starts with the journey to our ideal vision. What is this wonderful life going to look like for you? What is your vision for it? If you could be, do or have anything, what would it be? People simply don't take the time to think about that. And for no good reason, other than they are so involved in other aspects of their lives, many of which are not nearly as important as the time they could give to planning for greatness.

What do you want? Who do you want to be? I have spent a lot of time studying the success principles and ideas of the masters of personal development. And through my studies, I have learned that if you choose to be extraordinary, it is necessary to study with the people who are in the top of their field. Your journey to Imagineering your ideal life starts with searching for education and learning experiences. When I worked at a beautiful five star resort in San Diego as a concierge, I wanted to do an excellent job. All of my efforts in servicing the resort's guests resulted in the hotel receiving the most positive comment cards they ever received about any concierge who had ever worked there. I became the best because I gave my very best, 100%.

My goal was to make people happy on their vacation. That was my inspiration and vision to help make their experience easy and joyous for them and their families. Then, when I became an engineer, I rose to the top 10% of my engineering peers. I did this by modeling the very best engineers and working hard to understand the actual engineering principles and problem. I then focused on producing fast, high quality solutions. This was the vision for my journey. And it is a vision I have maintained through any and all of my jobs. The consistent belief that you can be the best, do the best, and try the best, will help to propel you through your journey and reach your ideal vision.

I took class after class, studying and working extremely hard to keep up with the ever-changing computer languages, architectural models, and systems engineering solutions. I had a vision, and that vision really paid off because I took the steps necessary to achieve a very solid career and excellent reputation.

While it is important to carry a strong and dedicated vision, vision without action will get you nowhere. It is like trying to run without moving your feet. Take your vision and implement it into your life. My vision was to become a successful engineer. So I fulfilled that vision by educating myself, studying the best of the best, and implementing these lessons into my life. But the lessons have to come from somewhere. Throughout your journey, you will learn from the experiences you have, but also from the education that you Imagineer and implement into your own life.

"We shape our buildings, thereafter they shape us."

—Winston Churchill

Importance of a Good Education

Visions come in many shapes and sizes, but it is vital to fulfilling your vision to find those shapes and sizes and make them fit into your own life. Only you can make your vision a reality. I knew at a young age that I had to be educated to fulfill my vision. That being said, I did everything I could to obtain the tools to make my game plan a reality.

In life, sometimes the experiences are free, and other times they cost more than you may ever anticipate. But a good education has a firm price tag and an invaluable benefit. The people you meet and the things you learn from being in a scholastic setting will have value that can never be appraised. Education offers you the tools and resources you will need to excel in life. Obviously there are people who have reached great success without education, but for every Michael Dell in the world, there are a million others that have failed without a proper classroom experience.

My Mom instilled in my sister and me the importance of getting a good college education. She believed in the importance of education because she always said, "no one can ever take that away from you." I am so grateful she and my Dad both believed so strongly in the value of a great education. I have them both to thank for my life success because without the focus on education, I would not be where I am today. My parents helped me as best they could financially to attend college. I also put myself through school any way I knew how. From taking on extra jobs to cutting back on my personal expenses, I made the necessary sacrifices to achieve my ideal life.

With vision comes sacrifice. To fill your tool belt with the tools you need to succeed, you may have to overcome difficult situations and obstacles. To fulfill my vision, I had to save every penny possible. Every time I was salivating for a big delicious steak or four-course meal, I revisited my ultimate vision and goal and it helped to keep me on my path. The same can be true for you. No one said fulfilling a vision is easy, and when the going gets tough, you have to remember why you are doing what you are doing and why you are giving up the four course meal or the strip.

"Your vision will become clear only when you can look into your own heart. Who looks outside dreams; who looks inside, awakens."

—CARL JUNG (FOUNDER OF ANALYTICAL PSYCHOLOGY)

Just Not Meant to Be

We have spoken a good deal about the importance of having a vision and imagining a life filled with success. I have always said a vision is a work in progress. You may be diligently headed in one direction, head down and focused on reaching your destination. And then life happens, and you have no choice but to change directions and re-plot your course. Life has a funny way of shifting, pulling, and pushing us in many different directions. One of my close friends once told me a moving story about his personal vision and how it took an unexpected turn.

I have a good friend named David who was an aerospace engineer in San Diego. We worked together at a gloomy and dark building, surrounded by dull colors and little excitement. One day we took a walk outside and the beautiful sun was shining. I looked at David and asked him, "Is this all there is?"

He started laughing and said, "I know" empathetic toward the discontent I was feeling when walking into that drab building each and every day. While we had well-paid jobs, we both felt like we were meant to do something more. We both had a bigger and better vision. David responded quietly, "Siobhan, all I can say is never turn down a job like the one that I turned down."

I was confused since this conversation occurred during a good economic time for engineering with many high-tech companies hiring engineers. I asked David to explain further. He quietly responded, "When

I graduated Stanford University, I interviewed at a small company of about six people who wanted to hire me. They offered me forty thousand shares of stock that were worth nothing at the time. I chose not to accept the job because it didn't seem very challenging."

I pronounced with such certainty, "David, you know what? That just was not your path."

He said, "But the shares and money were good."

I earnestly replied, "Some things are just not meant to be."

That's when he exclaimed, "The Company that I turned down was Google."

My eyes almost popped out of my head. I cannot describe the astonishment and laughter that poured out of me, tears rolling down my face. At that time Google stock had just hit four hundred dollars a share; David would have been worth more than $60 million dollars.

Who would have ever thought, David would have been one of Google's first employees. The company now employs over 20,000 people. My dear friend and I did share an enormous belly laugh that day trying to make sense of the ridiculousness of it all. David turned down what would be one of the most coveted jobs in America because it simply did not fit within his vision. He was dedicated and focused on a result, and knew that this small start up, while it may be lucrative and sexy on paper, was just simply not on his radar - it did not fit his vision.

Sometimes, you just do not know what life is going to throw at you. It all did work out in the end. David is now very successful in robotics and artificial intelligence in San Francisco and he loves what he does. It was the right path for him. Even though he may have a touch of regret because he is not a multi-millionaire today, when it comes down to it, he is successful, happy, and does not regret following his gut and foresight.

As we Imagineer our ideal life, we each will have a very specific path to reach our destination. But at the drop of a dime, that could change.

It is essential to maintain your vision through thick and thin, and never regret staying true to the game plan, always remembering that it is there for a reason. Simply put, some things are just not meant to be. But when you stay true to your dreams and your aspirations, you will never feel as if you made a mistake, because following your heart and staying true to your soul will offset even millions of dollars in stock options.

I Have to Go to School

Visions come in all sizes, both big and small. Whatever your vision may be, you have to remain determined and dedicated to it. Without determination and dedication to your vision, you never will fulfill its full potential. Even at a young age, I was determined to fulfill my vision of learning as much as I can and obtaining a great education.

When I was six years old, my family lived in Rockland County, New York with a beautiful view of the Hudson River. I had a happy playful childhood with the usual family dynamics. I was blessed to have one of the nicest most lovable mom's in the world. One morning while I was getting ready for first grade, I had missed the school bus because of a snowstorm.

We only had one car that my dad had already driven to work. So driving was not an option. My beautiful mother said, "It's okay. You can stay home from school and we'll spend the day together."

With utter urgency in my voice, I exclaimed, "Mommy, I HAVE to go to school." I didn't want to miss a thing that I was being taught and it was only first grade. But it was the world to me.

My mother, with determination put on her black rubber boots and bundled me up. Holding my hand the whole way, through the deep cold snow, she walked me the two and a half miles to my elementary school.

My precious mom knew how utterly important it was for me to get to school that day. Without a word of dismay, she kissed and hugged me goodbye at the school door, and walked back home. It is almost as if in my little six year old little body, I knew I had work to do and I was on it.

This is just one example of the substantial effect that upholding a strong vision through your journey will have. It keeps you focused, dedicated, and determined. It would have been easy to just stay in bed and succumb to my mother's advice and just stay home. But doing that was not part of the plan, and I was destined to get to school, no matter what the terrain may be. Thick or thin, rain or snow, stay true to your vision and allow it to prevail even in times of challenge. Obstacles will come often but it is up to you to stay dedicated to your vision and keep your journey going, one foot in front of the other.

Time for a Change

Sometimes even a steadfast and strong-minded person has trouble staying targeted on their vision. Not every day is inspired and motivated. Sometimes you just have to push through and maintain your focus, even when it seems impossible to do so.

Years ago, I attended an inspiring seven-day workshop titled "Breakthrough to Success" with Jack Canfield, one of the co-founders of the book series, "*Chicken Soup for the Soul.*" The workshop was full of like-minded individuals who aspired to create an extraordinary life for themselves. Jack taught us in a very dynamic learning environment numerous success principles and how to go about actually achieving our goals. It was exhausting but in an exhilarating type of way.

It was extremely difficult waking up on the following Monday morning to go into the office, especially after such an inspiring high-powered week. I opened my eyes and went to get up like I usually did, but I literally could not get out of bed. While completely healthy it was as though my inner soul was trapped. I laid there for a while giving myself a moment; recognizing this was a sign that something needed to change in my life. Now. I knew I enjoyed my job in engineering systems but that it was not my true calling. I lay there for quite a while pondering what I was going to actually do for the rest of my life.

Eventually I got up. I knew in my heart it was because I took the time to really listen to my inner voice, a voice that each of us has. At that distinct moment, I knew that I was really being true to myself. I realized that morning that I was truly passionate about helping people. How many of us never even take just a bit of quiet time to go inside ourselves to think about what we really want in life. It was a very profound moment when I stayed in bed and took that time for me.

The same should be true for you. We all have a strong inner vision, but it is our responsibility and our duty to find what that vision may be. It lies deep within each of us, but sometimes takes time to uncover. Find time each and every day to discover your true-life passions, as those are what will inevitably shape your vision. Whether it be lying in bed an extra five minutes or taking a fifteen-minute walk with nature each day, just find the time to do it for you.

When walking into work on that day after my morning breakfast filled with soul-searching, I knew I wanted more. It reverberated inside me, like a grand piano hitting a deep note. I began to feel like Fred Flintstone, punching a clock and answering to a horn that blows at the end of the day. So while I was grateful for my job and for the friendship and camaraderie of my colleagues, I knew that I was ready for a change. Even though I knew making such a bold career step would be scary and challenging, I was ready to live differently than Fred Flintstone who bellowed "Yabba Dabba Doooo" when the clock struck 5pm at the Slate quarry, and slid down a dinosaur. I was ready to find my own "Yabba Dabba Doooo."

The same should be true for you. When building a strong vision, it is crucial to remain dedicated to that vision and constantly assess and reassess. When you find yourself deviating from your overall game plan and moving in a direction that does not fit with your vision, it is vital to have the strength and self-belief to make the changes necessary to redirect and reposition yourself in the right direction.

Your Day-to-Day Life

To be a true visionary, you have to focus on all that life has to offer. You have to not only understand your surroundings, but also appreciate the fruits that fall off of life's vines. Remember, your daily life is your existence. Make each day an exceptional day.

Find things you are grateful for in your life and surround yourself with wonderful people with which to share those things. Focus on what you like. To achieve your goals, have picture boards, write things down and read them. Visualize your happiness and achievements. Just like the Olympic athletes do each and every day. Take a moment and lose yourself in dreaming. And most importantly, have fun. What you do for fun and what you love to do, make sure you stop and take the time to do it. Life can sometimes become a sheer race to the finish before we even know it.

You deserve to have the best possible life. I have listed below the seven key areas of your life. I want you to visualize and write down what you want these areas to look like for you in one year, three years, and five years. In working on this list, consider the interdependence between these areas; how each of these life elements intertwine. You cannot have a satisfying home life if you do not have a strong primary relationship. And you cannot have your ideal home life if you do not have the financial wherewithal to sustain it. But you can have happiness in all areas.

Putting pen to paper will help you formulate your ideal equation for Imagineering your perfect vision. Take time to review each of these areas of your life and think about not only what role they may play in your journey, but also how much time and effort you put into each piece of the puzzle…

- ➢ Home Life

- ➢ Relationships

- ➢ Financial

- ➢ Career

- ➢ Health

- ➢ Spiritual

- ➢ Playtime

It is vital to your vision to breakdown the fundamental parts of your life into its subsections. Once you do that, you can begin to understand the interdependence between your vision and your life. Take a look at each of the following sections of your life and consider what you would like your vision for each of these sub sections to be. Once you set defined boundaries for your vision, it will become easier to understand your ultimate goals.

The Power of Visualization

The power of visualization is quite a potent tool and is one of the keys to help you create your vision. Visualizing is the idea of looking toward your ideal future so that it can become a reality. It is practicing for the game in a sense. By taking time and picturing what you would like your life to look like, you will take essential steps towards reaching those goals. It all comes down to understanding where you want to be before you can start your journey to get there.

I once heard some exceptional speakers at an event in San Diego. I enjoyed all of the speakers very much. But the one speaker who really stood out is Ken Blanchard. Ken is the author of the incredible book *The One Minute Manager,* along with many other wonderful books. His genuine message of inspiration, leadership skills, and moving personal stories touched me to my very core.

After attending this seminar, I began to think about what the ultimate vision would be for my best life. I asked myself, "What job can I do that will allow me to travel all over the world and earn a living?" Then I saw the movie *Under the Tuscan Sun* starring Diane Lane. She played an author whose life in San Francisco was in tatters. Post-divorce, she numbly moved into a house in beautiful Tuscany, Italy and it was there that she discovered her essential self.

After seeing that movie, I realized that was the type of life I wanted to have. One that was simple with a focus on the thing that I love the most: writing. I share this because I want you to give thought to your definition of a happy life. Whether it is being a handyman, a flower shopkeeper, or even a CEO of your own company. There are no right and wrong answers. This is your life, your happiness, and your choice.

I have yet to achieve that dream of mine, but in every step of my life I always have a vision of where and what I ultimately want to be and what I want to achieve. I think it is important to zoom in on what you want. What is your life's vision? Do you spend time visualizing this ideal life each and every day? These are important questions to answer because they are vital steps to take to reach your dreams.

To reach your ultimate goals in life, you have to imagine and envision your future. It is sort of like great basketball players shooting a free throw to win the game. They have been in this position so many times before in their mind, visualizing stepping to the line and making the game winning free throw. Your imagination is one of the most powerful tools you have at your fingertips, so it is vital to your personal growth and success to visualize your destination on a daily basis. When you visualize these results, when the time comes to perform, you have been practicing for that moment for your entire life. It is familiar, manageable, and attainable.

Visualization is a way to prepare yourself for your journey. When you begin to visualize your journey, you will have the advantage of understanding the obstacles you may face, the course you will follow, and the easiest and most efficient way to optimize your ability to not only visualize success, but also reach it.

Visualization Boards

One great way of learning how to visualize is with vision boards. A vision board is simply a piece of poster board on which you tape pictures you've cut out of magazines, newspapers, or from the internet that represent your dreams. The pictures can be photos, images, words or anything that captures your interest and imagination. There are actually on-line tools now where you can create vision boards on your computer. I prefer to do it the old-fashioned way.

Come along side me and we will create your vision board. Here's how: collect a bunch of magazines and cut out pictures of what you want. What I mean by what you want is: your dream vacation, your dream house, your dream mate, your dream body, your dream anything and everything. Paste them on the board in any manner or direction.

Then put the board aside for a few hours. Go back to it and see what pictures and images you've assembled. What does it tell you about your dreams and hopes? It may be possible that you don't see images that spark your enthusiasm but you should work hard to find ones that do.

I remember cutting out a picture of my dream home on a beautiful golf course in Southern California. Now, five years later, I am living in that exact type of home. I feel extraordinarily blessed. And it all came down to working toward fulfilling my vision. Creating vision boards strengthens and focuses your desire. If you want a lean tone body, tack up a picture of a healthy fashion model on your board. If you love traveling, find the destination of your dreams and put up pictures of it.

I recommend that you visualize anything you want in the morning when you are first waking up, because you are still in a limbo state between being asleep and awake. I also want you to do it when you are tucked in for the night just before falling asleep. This is when you are most open to "out of the box" thinking. It is akin to making a movie of the life that you have always wished to star, but by first imagining it, and reviewing it when you start your day and when you end it. Only then can you wake-up inspired and go to bed fulfilled, knowing you are moving closer and closer to making your dreams a reality.

Ponder for a Moment

Imagine your life as a movie. Imagine you can be and do anything in and out of this world. No limitations. No fear. To help you move into that kind of imaginary world, think about some of your favorite movies for a moment. What are they and why did you enjoy them? In the world of movies, anything is possible. And why can't the same be true in your life? Why can't the things you only believe are possible be just that? Too often do we traverse our lives with boundaries and in a world filled with limitations. Your life is a limitless journey where you can not only define your ceilings, but also break through them time and time again.

I have a good friend named Kim who is a television producer. She gives keynote speeches around the country. Kim has this wonderful ability to run us through an exercise in which we create a movie of our ideal life. During this exercise, we utilize all five of our senses: sight, sound, smell, taste and touch.

Let's try it for moment. Sit down in a comfortable place and close your eyes. Imagine you are in the most beautiful place of your dreams. Is there a big blue ocean close by? Or are you in the cool green mountains? Now picture yourself in that place. What are you wearing? See yourself in this place. What do you look like? Are you lean and tone, happy, and smiling? Who is beside you, if anyone? What are you doing in this beautiful place? Are you walking, relaxing, etc?

Now, just for a moment take a look around and take a deep breath. Imagine you have made the life of your dreams come true. You are completely at peace. When you are ready you can slowly open your eyes. You have just made a movie with your mind. Take note of the clip you create, and replay it each and every day you wake up.

This example of visualization can be a powerful tool that you can implement into your own life. For example, in my movie, I am twenty feet from the big beautiful blue Pacific Ocean in my beach house. I am slender and lean, barefoot, wearing a blue tank and loose fitting white jean shorts. I am lying on a lounge chair in my Del Mar Beach home. I can picture the furniture, the big fluffy white couches with bright colorful pillows. I hear the crash of the ocean waves. I can taste the sea air. I smell a huge vase full of multi-colored magnificent flowers that just arrived from one of my best friends in New Jersey congratulating me on another bestselling book. I can see and feel how happy I am. The warm ocean breeze brushes across my face. I can see awards hanging on the walls in my office from all the books, speaking engagements, and philanthropic work I have done. This is my dream. When I play the movie in my mind ever so clearly, I am happy and at peace.

By scripting your own movie, you take the first steps in creating an illustration of your ideal life. When Imagineering your ideal life, it is not about the big things that make a difference, it is about the small steps you take on a daily basis that eventually add up to make a gigantic difference in your life. This chapter is one about small steps, all leading up to a grand finale that inevitably has a lasting influence. We spent a sizeable amount of time discussing the importance of your personal vision. It is a reflection of your goals, forethought, and desire for your future life.

This vision should be driven by your imagination, wisdom, and life experience. Your imagination is a powerful resource, as it pushes your limits and drives you to reach for pinnacles that may otherwise seem unreachable. Focus on the exercises in this chapter to ensure your imagination is in tip top shape and push your vision to extremes you never thought possible. Because if Walt Disney can create one of the largest companies in the world, then Imagineering your ideal life is just a little vision with a lot of imagination away.

Snippets: Computer Science

Most Powerful Computer

Your brain is significantly more powerful than any computer. Believe it. The average desktop model can execute 100 billion instructions per second, while the human brain is capable of processing a quantum more per second of information. It has been discovered that 2% - 4% of your processing is done through the conscious mind and 96% - 98% of your thought processing is done through the unconscious mind.

Computer Disk Drive

The world's first computer hard drive, unveiled by IBM in 1956, was the size of a walk-in closet, equipped with 16 kilobytes of memory. The disk drive had a capacity of five megabytes. To think that we can just drive over to the local Best Buy and fit a disk drive, once the size of a huge closet, right into our pocket.

Apple Vision

One of the most incredible visionaries of our time is the engineering genius Steve Jobs (February 24, 1955 – October 5, 2011) who co-founded Apple Inc. Known as one of the first pioneers of the personal computer revolution, running his many companies, and responsible for overseeing the development of the iMac, iTunes, iPhone and iPad. Steve will be remembered as a fiery visionary with an amazing ability to pick himself up when life pushed him down. He is an inspiration and example to us all that our dreams can come true if we truly believe in them.

Plus Up

Review what you wrote for the previous chapter's 'Plus-Up' exercise. What did you write down for what inspires you? Is what inspires you part of that vision? If not, how can you make it part of your vision?

> ➤ What do you envision for your ultimate life?

> ➤ What do you think about and focus on each day?

> ➤ What would make you the happiest in all areas of your life?
> Home Life
> Relationships
> Financial
> Career
> Health & Wellness
> Spiritual
> Playtime

➤ You have a choice to envision your life. What is getting in the way of your taking the time or having the courage to envision your ideal life?

➤ Finish this sentence. If I could have _____, my life would be complete.

➤ What do I need to relinquish to have that ultimate vision?

3

The Blueprint

LAYING THE FOUNDATION

"If you have built castles in the air, your work may not be lost; that is where they should be. Now put the foundations under them."

—HENRY DAVID THOREAU

Throughout this book, I have provided you with the groundwork to create a successful and prosperous life. But with every magnificent structure comes the most important part...the blueprint. No matter how big your castle may be, without the proper foundation, it will inevitably crumble to the ground. This chapter centers on giving you those vital tools you will need to lay a concrete foundation that you can build your skyscrapers of success on top of a strong foundation.

Science of Systems Engineering

There are many ways to blueprint your ideal life. And as this chapter progresses, we will talk about plenty of them. But first, it is important to understand the difference between architecting and blueprinting. The blueprint is the thinking and the planning, while the architect is the building and the doing. As an architect, you have to implement your blueprint to make it a reality. But as a planner, it must be your goal to lay down a game plan to imagineer your ideal life.

Consider the concept of the systematic engineering approach. Wikipedia defines systematic engineering as "an interdisciplinary field of engineering that focuses on how complex engineering projects should be designed and managed over the life cycle of the project. Issues, such as logistics, the coordination of different teams, and engineering become more difficult when dealing with large, complex projects. Systems engineering deals with work-processes and tools to handle such projects."

So how can you apply this concept of systematic engineering to your own life? The fact of the matter is that each of us can take a concrete science and use it to map out your life plan. The fields of engineering and architecture vary significantly. Engineering is not subjective. It is concrete. For example, in the formula "$3x = 6$", "x" will always equal 2. 100 out of 100 times. That's what I enjoy about engineering—the idea that we work in definites.

However, on the flipside, architecture is very subjective and cannot be based simply on formulas. There is abstract and creativity, which go a long way to formulating a result. So the challenge comes in finding the balance between the abstract and the concrete, and that is what we will focus on as we discuss how to blueprint your ideal life through the paradigm of systematic engineering.

"Therefore O Students study mathematics and do not build without foundation."

—LEONARDO DA VINCI

My Engineering Profession

In Systems Engineering, before we even begin to develop a single line of code, we write out clearly defined requirements. That is, we define what exactly the foundation for the rest of the system will be. The place to start building your ultimate life is to clearly identify the ultimate life you want to create for yourself. Only then can you begin to design your life. If we do not take the time to sit down and clearly think through the requirements for our life design, we will end up going through life without any clear direction. Almost like a ship sailing without a captain or even a clear destination.

As a systems engineer, I have gotten very comfortable with all types of foreign jargon I never even knew existed. It was just like learning a new language over the years. However, many of the terms I use in my everyday life are not only relevant, but can also be used as examples for each of us to help improve all of our lives. While writing this book, I also work as a Senior Principal Systems Engineer, responsible for designing, developing, and testing systems at a 100,000-person worldwide Aerospace/Defense Company. I want to share my professional mindset to help you get your life on track and move you in the right direction towards building your ultimate life.

Consider how the following engineering terminology can apply to your own life:

➢ **Requirement** - Something that is required; is a necessity. What are the basic requirements for your life?

➤ **Methodology** - A body of practices and procedures used in a discipline. How are you going to structure your days?

➤ **Process** - A series of actions, changes of functions that bring about a result. What action steps are you going to take to get to your goals?

Throughout your journey to blueprint your ideal life, you will find that you inevitably have to answer the questions above. Without clarity surrounding what you need in life, how you will experience life, and how you will reach your goals, there is no way you will create a useful blueprint. So start there, answering the questions above so that you can begin shading in the lines and building a structure for your blueprint.

> *"I am only a pencil in the hand of God."*
>
> —MOTHER TERESA

Pencil it in...

Your blueprint is fluid, and always changing and moving around. What works one day may not work the next. Remember that you should write your blueprint with a metaphorical pencil maintaining the basic knowledge that as life changes, so will your goals and aspirations.

In architecture school, I had an electrical eraser and used it many times. In fact, I probably went through more erasers than pencils during my time in school. When conceptualizing a blueprint for our life, do not be afraid to change directions often. This is your life we are talking about, so it is okay to make a mistake, or decide a specific path is better than the one you may be on. Even more so, my guess is you may rethink your destination time and time again, so do not be afraid to take out your eraser and use it liberally and often.

Before you can begin creating a magnificent blueprint for your life, it is vital to take some time and prepare for this arduous task. Think about those things in your life that truly illuminate and light your soul on fire. Think about those aspects that will create a meaningful foundation. Your foundation has to be strong, so remember to tie it into the strongest parts of your fiber. You must prepare for living this extraordinary life, and you can do that by taking baby action steps each day toward your ultimate vision. The Egyptian pyramids were not built in a day. The task was immense and took a lot of planning. The same is true for Imagineering your ideal life--one brick at a time,

Affirmations

It is important to affirm your decisions and actions. The concept of telling yourself certain things in life are true and valid will allow you the opportunity to internally design a fruitful life. As you navigate your blueprint, use affirmations liberally and act as if they are already true. Slowly, you will begin to live the life you affirm.

Maintaining a positive attitude and envisioning and projecting your life's goals are vital to achieving success and a prosperous life. The process of affirmation will help lead to confirmation. Meaning, once you put it out there, it will become easier to reach. Those who did not first believe in and personally affirm that they could achieve greatness never did.

Before you even can begin creating a blueprint for your ideal life, you have come to terms with the goals you want to reach as you traverse the terrain. And when formulating these goals, it is crucial that you have confidence and affirm your ability to achieve them. If you start with a negative attitude or do not believe that you will get where you want to go, you never had a chance to begin with. Affirm your goals, reinforce your abilities, and when choosing the format of your blueprint, remember that you have achieved, can achieve, and you will achieve.

The Power of Mentors

The power of people is truly an amazing phenomenon. Learning from one another and taking those lessons and implementing them into your own life are at the heart of this book. It is vital to your personal success to surround yourself with those people that push you to greatness and set examples along the way. Each and every one of us needs our own personal cheerleading section, pushing us on through challenges and obstacles. We also need the type of people that will not just cheerlead, but also put on the helmets and battle with us.

Always remember that there is somebody who has already done what you want to do (or at least a proximate version of your plan). Find people who achieved what you desire to accomplish and model them. Successful people also love to share their insights. I have numerous mentors who have guided me in my many endeavors. That is what great coaches do and I've studied an enormous number of successful people, each of whom has some wisdom to share, but more importantly, each of whom had a mentor and a confidant who helped guide them through their own journey to success.

My father always told me good people at the top of their field want to surround themselves with good people and are usually always happy to share their wisdom. Through the years, I learned my dad was absolutely correct. At some point in their lives, even the most successful people in the world were given advice and direction.

Someone went out of his or her way to provide these people with helpful tools to reach greatness. So why would they not want to pay it forward and help another to reach their own personal goals. Surround yourself with the smartest and most talented people you know, and use them as resources and tools to help you create your ideal blueprint.

What you Watch on TV and What you Read

As you travel through each and every day of your life, you will meet new people and have millions of different experiences. So much of what you do on a daily basis affects how you think and how you feel. In addition to the people we meet, we all spend some part of our day either in front of a television or engaged in a book, magazine, or newspaper. The things we read and watch have profound effects on how we behave and how we blueprint. That being said, it is essential to shaping our ideal life to consider what we put in front of our eyes and ears.

What goes into your psyche is what you think about. You want to ingest good and valuable input and to surround yourself with positive inspiration. You can and do have the power to choose how you live your life. You are the captain of your ship.

The process of learning and educating yourself is an endless one. We never can know enough and we should all spend some time each and every day striving and looking to discover the next lesson. I have incorporated the teachings of some of the greatest scholars and thinkers of our time, as I know their guidance and advice can help me build a useful blueprint for my own life. We live in the age of information, with almost any fact or lesson a short drive or a few clicks away.

There is never a shortage of things to learn when it comes to all of the communication mediums with which we are surrounded. Find the ones that resonate with you, whether it is books, magazines, newspaper, television, and the Internet, and use this authoritative wealth of information to help sculpt your blueprint for the life that you choose to live.

The Power of Asking

A powerful tool to help you build your life is called "Asking." No one knows what you want until you ask. Mark Victor Hansen and Jack Canfield's marvelous book *The Aladdin Factor* discusses the power of asking and goes into depth on how important it is to just "ask" for what you want. I highly recommend it.

For example, when I check into a beautiful hotel, I always ask for the upper floor with the nicest view and I usually get it. I also ask if I can have concierge privileges and they usually give them to me. It only takes a moment to ask for what I want. Hotel staff are usually happy to help and accommodate guests to ensure that their stay is a pleasant one.

The Big Gun

The simple task of taking time to speak to people can pay enormous dividends in your ability to lay a meaningful and concrete foundation in your life. Whether you want to become the CEO of a Fortune 500 Company, or the guy pitching a product to that company, interacting with people can open up doors that will nurture your garden and help blueprint a prosperous master plan.

When I first started working in engineering I travelled a lot. I like meeting people and I enjoy hearing their stories so I would always talk to people on airplanes. You just never know what someone may teach you. As I boarded a plane on my way home to San Diego on a particular trip, I was unexpectedly upgraded to first class. I sat next to a very nice gentleman and we began light chitchat soon after take-off.

After sharing a very nice dinner my new friend said to me, "You know, there are probably fifty people on this plane right now that work for me."

I said, "Wow, what do you do?"

He said, "I am head of SPAWAR in San Diego."

SPAWAR (Space and Naval Warfare Systems Command) is the Navy's designated technical authority for Command, Control, Communications, Computers, Intelligence, Surveillance & Reconnaissance (**C4ISR**), business information, technology, and space systems. It is also one of the largest companies in San Diego, employing thousands.

I was blown away that this nice man was the majordomo of this incredible company. While we continued chatting and enjoying our delightful first class environment on the airplane, I asked him, "If you could teach any one thing to someone like me who is first starting out, what would it be?"

He asked, "How often do you go up to the higher-ups and talk to them?"

I said, "I just interviewed a director at the company I worked for and asked her how she was able to achieve her current senior position."

He said, "Do you ever just go in and 'shoot the breeze' with them?" He did use a much more Navy-like term though.

I took his advice to heart. Rather than always talk business, I just talk a minute or two to hear about the outside life of my colleagues. It has helped me to form many friendships with my colleagues as well as with the senior level executives at the company. We are all just people and I truly feel it is very important to form good relationships and genuine friendships.

I learned a valuable lesson that day on the plane. Take time for small talk and become genuinely interested in people's lives outside of work. Everyone has a life and we are all on our own journey. Take a moment to share a kind word. Take the time to ask a colleague how he or she is doing with care and interest. You may be pleasantly surprised of the friendships you form. But even more helpful will be the lessons you may learn from the experiences of others. When formulating your ideal blueprint, it is vital to include the lessons you learn from others.

So many times in life we are inspired and motivated to reach for a goal because of what we see or hear from other people. Maybe you heard a story about a malnourished dog and then decided to volunteer at The Humane Society. Or maybe a close friend was stricken with a terrible illness, which inspired you to go to medical school to help find a cure. Each of these goals starts with a simple conversation, but eventually becomes a significant part of your blueprint. Communicate often and engage in conversation generously as you never know the profound effects a simple "Hello, how are you doing?" may have on your life and the lives of others.

The Hardware Store

"Don't go to the hardware store for apples" my dad taught me. Meaning if a person is not able to help you then don't seek their advice. Look in the right places. If you don't have a good feeling about the advice or the person offering it, go somewhere else. Go to the places where like-minded people hang out.

For example, I wanted to become an excellent public speaker so I joined two Toastmasters clubs that met once a week in San Diego. It was the best thing I could have ever done in order to work on my speaking skills. Toastmasters International focuses on helping people with self-confidence, speaking, leadership, and listening skills. This exceptional organization has more than 260,000 members in over 12,500 clubs in 113 countries.

I highly recommend joining a club. Many shy away because they have a fear of speaking; but Toastmasters helps you overcome this fear. Even if you are an excellent speaker, you can still learn a great deal. At Toastmasters meetings and events, I was always around people who were kind and driven to better themselves.

Just like you and me.

Success Reminders

Blueprinting a meaningful life is like a garden that needs constant attention. From planting seeds, to watering, to ensuring it receives enough sunshine on a daily basis, a garden is a constant work in progress.

I like to think that reminding yourself of your accomplishments will help push you to building your ideal life. Giving yourself daily success reminders is a fantastic way to provide your garden with the nourishment it may need. Even more so, at times when you are designing a blueprint for your life, you often face obstacles and walls. If reminders of how you previously overcame challenges surround you, you will be encouraged to push on and find the accomplishments that you reach for each and every day.

Reminding yourself of your successes and accomplishments is very motivating. Place reminders around your home and you will find yourself thinking, "Hey, if I can do that, I can do anything." For example, I always carry around my Arizona State University alumni key chain on my key ring. The reason for that is it reminds me that if I could graduate from ASU's Architecture school, I can achieve anything I choose to achieve.

These small reminders of your victories in your life do not have to be significant or glaring. In fact, sometimes less is more. A small but representative souvenir of your journey to overcoming or accomplishing should instill a sense of pride and ability to keep going and get the job done.

When blueprinting, you will naturally set a series of goals you are striving to reach. Sometimes you will be faced with obstacles as you navigate your blueprint. However, that extra push that may come from your history of success can often make the difference between achieving or not. Celebrate your victories often and never hesitate to reminisce about all that you have done.

One Line at a Time

As a systems engineer, currently my daily task is to help integrate and test a complex intelligent computer system within a team of very talented engineers. It can certainly seem like a daunting task at times. The same can ring true when building a blueprint for your life. The idea of designing the next thirty of forty years of your life can be overwhelming, but it does not have to be. The Egyptian Pyramids started with one stone…and then another, until they stood hundreds of feet high. When blueprinting your life-plan, remember that you have to start at the beginning and move one stone, or step, at a time.

Earning my architecture degree was one of the most challenging times in my life. The school I attended in Tempe, Arizona is one of the most competitive in the country. Only 48 students of the hundreds of applicants are selected each year. The school expected nothing but excellence. If your grades fell below a 3.0 GPA, you were out. One night I was at the condominium I was sharing with my roommates, stressing out.

I needed to design a newspaper building including blueprints, renderings, and a large-scale model. It was an enormous amount of work for just one project. I worked feverishly knowing, once again, that I faced another all-nighter. It was already 9pm when I thought to myself, "Would I finish?" At that moment the phone rang and it was my father calling from New York City.

I said, "Hi Daddy, how is everything?"

He said, "Hi Peach, I woke up and I thought that I should give you a call to see how you were doing?"

I proceeded to pour out my fear of not finishing my project, how scared I was about how much I had to do, and how I didn't know how I would finish.

Just by having my dad listening to me and hearing his words of encouragement were extremely helpful. Then he said something to me that, to this day, when confronted with a disarmingly monstrous task, I still say to myself: *"All you can do is just one line at a time, just keep saying that to yourself. One line at a time. One line at a time."*

I must have repeated that one sentence to myself three thousand times that night but it got me through what would have been a horrific night. When you are faced with a daunting task as you design and build your extraordinary life, and you may be getting stuck, repeat to yourself, "One line at a time, I can do it!"

Designing Your Blueprint

With all of this said regarding the groundwork to building a blueprint, it is time to begin designing your ideal version of it. Start with a blank sheet of unlined paper. In Architecture, before you begin the blueprint you need to build a schematic. A schematic is a framework for what you are building. It is the skeleton to which you eventually attach your flesh. For example, let's say you are designing a house. You begin with a blank sheet of paper, and then draw a series of circles, each circle representing a room. The relationship of rooms is placed by each other in areas, as you want them to relate to one another.

To correlate this technique in designing your life, ask yourself what areas are most important to you? What is your schematic for your blueprint? Remember, when you have a clearly defined path of where you ultimately want to be, your chances of getting there are much greater. This is true no matter what time in your life it is. Begin to draw these circles on your blueprint and fill them in. These should represent the most important pieces of your life. From family, to friends, to work, to income, to philanthropy, create as many circles as necessary to create a strong schematic.

The next step is to ask yourself, "What is the life I want to create for beautiful, wonderful me?" Look at each of your circles and begin to fill in what you have accomplished in each area. Do you have a family? A good job? Plenty of friends? Write all of these down. This will enable you to understand what you have, but also bring to light what you may want to improve.

After reviewing all that you have, it is time to consider what goals you would like to achieve. Within these circles, begin to write down your goals. Perhaps you are not married and want to build a family. Write it down. Maybe you would like a raise or promotion. Write it down. Maybe you do not volunteer enough. Write it down. Now your schematic is beginning to have a little meat to it. You should be able to look at your blueprint and in just a few seconds, inventory the most vital pieces of your life, what you have accomplished in those pieces, and what you are striving for. That is the purpose of a blueprint.

Let your thoughts flow freely. If you are struggling with this, no problem as you have planted a seed that your subconscious will manifest and soon you will burst forth all that is deep inside you. Devote time each day to think about this; it may take some time. Each of us has a blueprint of our most desired treasures and adventures and, of course, our most desired life, inside of us. By doing this exercise it will allow you to cultivate the blueprint for your ideal life.

Some people have discovered that they filled up the blank page with many different and diverging thoughts and ideas. Ideas shot in from every angle, almost like a fire hose from your heart. The sky is the limit here. "No holds barred!" There are no restrictions or rules on what you can put on your blank piece of paper.

Seeing what you want and understanding what truly matters to you is important. Reading it on paper makes it so much more tangible that it should give you a stronger sense that a new life is possible.

If you're having trouble developing your blueprint, don't worry. Some people can access this information internally more quickly; for others, this is a longer process. But it doesn't matter. The process, in and of itself, is a critical part of the journey. Try not to put too much pressure on yourself. If you're not feeling it today, put it down and come back to it tomorrow. Try again. Have fun with it. This is just life and when you are ready you will be ready. Be easy on yourself. As the old saying goes, "When the student is ready, the teacher will appear."

When building your blueprint, keep it light. If you feel yourself getting too serious or wrapped up in it all again, step back and pull out another blank sheet of paper to begin your fresh new blueprint. What you've put on paper should demonstrate that you are now at the precipice of an unlimited attainable and spectacular fulfilled life. Identifying what is most important to you in life is the key here.

Putting pen to paper will help you define pieces of your blueprint. It will also help you to be accountable to your goals. Once they are on paper, you always have the opportunity to look back and evaluate not only what you are doing, but also how far you have come on your journey.

Your Comfort Zone

When building a blueprint for your life, you have to understand what makes you comfortable and what makes you uncomfortable. That is part of your journey to blueprint your ideal life. Too many people design their lives based on their comfort zones. While it is valuable to play to your strengths, putting yourself in uncomfortable positions is vital to your growth and to pushing yourself to reaching your goals.

Do you spend more time in your comfort zone or your uncomfortable zone? The majority of people spend 80% of their time in their comfort zone when they should actually be spending 70% of the time in their uncomfortable zone. Why? It's in the uncomfortable zone where you learn and grow.

As you build your blueprint, consider what places you in your uncomfortable zone? What makes you anxious, nervous, or fearful? For example, many people find discomfort in social situations like parties where they might meet new people and feel that they may be exposed in some way. Other common examples are a fear of test taking, fear of speaking engagements, and fear of one-on-one moments. Once you recognize that you are in an uncomfortable zone, think of it as an opportunity to grow. Much of your schematic may even reflect your desire to improve these uncomfortable areas of your life. The circles that really stress you out will generally be ripe areas to improve. And just by knowing that a specific experience is stressful and challenging will often times help you take the necessary steps to remedy those issues.

Failure is Okay

There will be times in your life when you are going to fail. As you create a blueprint and imagineer your ideal life, you have to factor in a learning curve as well as the possibility for falling short of your goals. Now on paper the thought of failure just sounds awful. But in life, failure is not only part of it, but also a helpful and useful tool if used correctly.

Everyone experiences successes and failures. It does not matter who you are or what you do, at some point, you will not hit the bull's-eye. But that is ok. Why? Because with failure, comes valuable lessons and experiences. You will learn what to do and what not to do the next time. When you fail, try to pat yourself on the back because you took action. And then learn something as a result.

But it does not stop there. Failure is not just about learning lessons. Failure is about looking at things from a different perspective. Sometimes what seems like a mistake can actually be an overwhelming triumph. Consider the renowned "Leaning Tower of Pisa" located in Pisa, Italy. It may seem like a failure since the Tower did not stay straight up as planned. But consider that millions travel each year just to see this freestanding leaning bell tower.

How many would do the same if the tower had not failed and leaned? The tower began leaning shortly after construction began in 1173. The ground first began to sink after the first three stories were built. Today, the tower leans 4.8 yards (4.4 meters) out of line. It is quite a sight to see. As an architectural structure, some may deem it a failure. But as a tourist attraction and a piece of Italian history, it is one of the greatest successes around.

While it is crucial to learn from each of our mistakes, you should never forget that some mistakes simply do not need to occur. Errors are caused in many different ways, some we have control over, and some we do not. The key to building a successful blueprint is to avoid the unnecessary failures, such as the ones that are caused by improper planning, rushing, or human error.

An excellent example of failing to plan is the Tacoma Washington Bridge disaster. The bridge was opened to traffic on July 1, 1940. It was made up of a pair of mile long (1600 meter) suspension bridges. The bridge was the third longest suspension bridge just behind the Golden Gate Bridge and George Washington Bridge. High winds caused the bridge to move vertically, thereby earning the bridge the nickname *Galloping Gertie*.

Four months after opening a dramatic wind induced the bridge to structural collapse. Thankfully no one was hurt. A review of what happened revealed a lack of planning. The failure did have a lasting effect on engineering and science. *Galloping Gertie* influenced the study of aerodynamics-aeroelastics in bridge building and has been key in the design of the world's greatest long-span bridges since 1940.

Unfortunately, history repeats itself time and time again. Another failure caused by poor design was the Hyatt Regency Hotel in Kansas City, Missouri. The fourth floor bridge was suspended directly over the second floor bridge with the third floor walkway set off to the side, several meters away from the other two. Construction issues led to a subtle but flawed design change that doubled the load on the connection between the fourth floor walkway support beams and the tie rods carrying the weight of the second floor. This design could barely handle the weight of the structure itself, much less hundreds of guests. The connection failed and both walkways crashed onto the lobby killing 114 people and injuring more than 200 others.

Proper planning could have probably prevented all of these disasters. Although some things are clearly out of our control, proper planning may help prevent your potential life's debacles. At the end of the day, mistakes and failures are part of life. They will inevitably occur, even if you are the greatest planner in the world. Sometimes life just throws you an unscalable wall, or an unreachable object.

But how you deal with those failures and how you turn negatives into positives will be the difference between being good and becoming great. At times it comes down to proper planning to avoid pitfalls that may be present throughout your journey.

Other times, it may be about changing your perspective and looking at things in a positive manner. Not all things that seem like failures actually are. There are gifts with each and every mistake or error, and finding those gifts is a valuable part of life. Regardless, you cannot avoid the occasion where you fall short of your goals, so when creating a blueprint for your ideal life, factor in the bumps that will inevitably knock you off course. And once they arise, diligently work to turn a negative into a positive.

Time to Blueprint

Blueprinting your ideal life may seem like a daunting task at first, but it does not have to be. Think of all the amazing man-made architectural triumphs across the world. Each of these beautiful achievements started with an idea, design, and some sketches. The same is true with building and Imagineering your ideal life. It has to start with a sketch, and putting pencil to paper. This chapter has provided you with the tools to do just that. Before you can begin to blueprint an ideal life, you have to first inventory where you are in your life and what your life consists of. Who are your friends? Who are your mentors? What does your daily routine consist of? These are all vital questions to answer before you begin blueprinting.

Next, you have to understand the blueprinting process. By starting with a schematic and penciling in the pieces of your personal puzzle, you will begin to inventory the fibers of your life. This will help you find out what you have, and also survey what you may need. Once you take a 10,000-foot review of your life and create a strong blueprint, it will act as a guiding light, a tall and bright lighthouse guiding you through the high seas.

Staying motivated through this difficult and arduous task can be tough, but using your mentors and relying on your success reminders will keep you motivated and dedicated to your vision. Blueprinting is the planning to your action. This is your life. You only have one and it is your duty to both yourself and the people with which you surround yourself to live it to the fullest and be the best version of you that you can be. Blueprint soon, reassess often, and never forget that you have the tools and resources to imagineer your ideal life.

Snippets: Computer Breakthroughs

Birth of The Internet

While working for the Department of Defense, Joseph Licklider was looking for a way to link computers around the country in order to control radar defense systems. He actually developed what we now know as the Internet between 1962 and 1965. The worldwide web first began life as a computer network, and the first computers connected were at the University of California in Los Angeles and the Stanford Research Institute located in Menlo Park, California.

Information Sharing

The Internet, as we know it today, began working by allowing computers to communicate with one another via phone line. Never before had computers been able to communicate in this way before. Broadband technology meant that fiber optic cables could carry much greater amounts of information because the cables had enough capacity to carry both the telephone signal and the computer signal. Pretty nifty!

First Website

On August 6, 1991, the first website was launched on the Internet at CERN (European Organization for Nuclear Research). It explained how to set up a web server as well as the concept of the World Wide Web. Sir Timothy John Berners-Lee is an MIT professor, computer scientist, and the person who can be credited for inventing the World Wide Web.

Plus Up

The following questions are to get you thinking and focused on what and how you want to live your life. Before we close this chapter, I want to give you some basic and fundamental questions that you can ask yourself to help build a blueprint for your life. Consider the following questions and answer each one before you begin to design your blueprint.

➢ How would you live each day if you could, any way you wanted?

➢ How would you map out your life?

➢ What would be your desired lifestyle?

➢ What kind of life would you design to be most happy, fulfilled and at peace?

➢ You are in control of your destiny. What do you want your destiny to be?

➢ What one step can you take today to start moving in that direction?

➢ We all have a beautiful blank canvas in front of us; we can be and do anything we set our mind to. What was your life pencil meant to draw?

➢ What legacy will you be most happy to leave behind?
[Note: Look fear in the eye and go for it anyway.]

4
The Architect
YOU ARE THE MASTER BUILDER

"Think of yourself as on the threshold of unparalleled success. A whole clear glorious life lies before you; Achieve, Achieve."

—ANDREW CARNEGIE

You are the Architect of your Life

Each of us is the architect for our own life. This is one of the most empowering beliefs we can have for ourselves. Just as an architect plans, designs, and builds beautiful homes, skyscrapers, and buildings, you too can be an architect, designing, building, and implementing a fantastic blueprint into your every day life. This chapter focuses on unlocking your innermost ability to construct and develop an extraordinary life.

You are the architect and engineer of your life. You have the ability to not only design, but also build the life of your dreams. And here is the best part: once you build your dream life, in true architect fashion, you can redesign, change, and improve different aspects of it. You have the tools, the resources, and the power to mold and sculpt the perfect life for you.

Think Tank

Consider the idea of a think tank. This is the general concept of a group of people coming together to achieve a common goal through bouncing ideas off of one another and looking at different angles to solve complicated issues. A think tank represents the idea that two heads are better than one, and when it comes to architecting your own life, a think tank can be a valuable resource.

While I was attending Northeastern University in Boston studying Mechanical Engineering, I would take my nightly five-mile run around the Charles River. Each night I would pass by the Massachusetts Institute of Technology. Unbeknownst to me at the time, I eventually found out I was also running past the school's "think tank." At nineteen years old, I had never heard of such a concept or place before, but intrinsically I knew it was a place where extraordinary ideas originated, and even more importantly, a place that could benefit each of us.

After finding out I was circling one of the greatest "Think Tank's" in the world, as I continued my run, I wondered with fascination what actually went on inside there? I could not help myself but to think what incredible minds were at work? I later did more research on the subject and found out that particular "think tank" was a place where some of the leading professors in the world dedicated themselves to finding solutions to the most universal of problems. Through coming together, they had the exciting opportunity to solve issues that may otherwise be unsolved.

I ask myself today why are we not all contemplating and designing our lives in our mind's eye just like they do in a "think tank?" How many of us take even a few minutes to brainstorm, to plan, to dream of all the places we want to go, undertake all the accomplishments we want to attain and consider all the possibilities that are open to us?

Implementing the concept of a "think tank" into your own life will help you gain a better understanding of not only the blueprint for your life, but also how to transform this blueprint into a reality.

> *"I am an Engineer, I serve mankind*
> *by making dreams come true."*
>
> —ANONYMOUS

Energy Power Source

We all have a certain type of energy inside of us. The most successful people in the world are those that draw people in to their energy and their vibe. As an architect of your own life, it is vital to build a positive energy and a luminous light around yourself. By doing this, you attract people that will help to build your life up, as opposed to put cracks in the foundation and even bring you down.

I recently attended a speaking class with one of my greatest mentors, Barbara DeAngelis, best-selling author and one of the most influential teachers of our time in the field of personal growth and relationships. She is a pioneer in the field of personal transformation, which unfortunately, is a foreign concept to many. Even to me at the time.

At the event, one of the exercises she had us do was to construct seven sentences and present those sentences for about a minute or so to the group. There were sixteen people in the class, broken down into groups of four when we started the exercise, which was being videotaped at the time.

Barbara then said, "I want you to deliver this speech in a different language."
I was thinking to myself, "What, French?"

Then she explained, "What I mean is say it in tones like 'la-la-la'.

I wasn't quite sure how I was going to do it but I uttered "Ba-ba-boo, ba-ba-boo, ba-ba-boo." After I had expressed those sounds, a tear came to my eye. It was a very inspirational speech I was giving, yet I wasn't saying anything.

The people in my group said, "Oh my goodness, you have to play this back for the whole class to see." We played it back, and the class and I hung on every word that I was saying. I was saying nothing, but after I was done one woman yelled out, "I'll buy it," because it was so genuine. I was surprised because I was so much better at saying nothing than saying words with content. That is what Barbara wanted to teach us—that it's not always about what you say, but how you say it and whether you believe in yourself and your message.

The purpose of this story is to demonstrate that each of us gives off a vibe. The way we carry ourselves and the way we present ourselves to the outside world speaks monumentally about who we are and what we are about. What kind of vibe do you give off? Is it high energy, calm energy or negative energy? Do people like to be around you? Are you genuine? People can feel your intent and often times make a snap judgment based on the energy you emanate. Who are you going to be? What is your ultimate who?

We only have this one life to live. We each are the master builders and creators for how we choose to design and build it. There is no one in the world that will take responsibility for your life like you will, and the idea of architecting your own life is about finding those things that make you tick, and building a life centered on those nuggets. Each of us has our own unique energy that we derive from the pieces of our puzzle and projecting that energy and vibe in a positive manner to the world. Not only will that energy draw people to us, but it will also help recruit the ideal people to chip in and help you build a fruitful and successful life.

Step Out Of Yourself

At times, it can be so easy to get completely wrapped up in our lives doing and doing that we often get lost in our own actions and forget to take time to inventory our lives for a moment. This means to truly become aware of our daily choices, endeavors, and interactions. Sometimes it is more important to play the role of the director or producer, than it is to be the actor. Meaning, taking the time to look at the 10,000-foot view of our lives and take a step back to account for where we are and what we are doing. Literally, it is almost like taking a break from you just for a few moments. When architecting your life, this is a vital step to take on a daily basis.

When a builder lays bricks for a house, every so often, he takes a few steps back from his work to ensure the bricks are flush and straight. If just one brick is crooked and the builder does not notice, that may result in stacks and stacks of unbalanced and unlevel bricks. The same is true in life. You always have to step back and make sure you are level and balanced while architecting your ideal life.

Who is responsible for your life? Ultimately, you and you alone are responsible for your life and the choices you make. All of your decisions up to this point have shaped your destiny. Inevitably, you build your life with the decisions and actions that you choose to make. And with those decisions comes the responsibility to constantly inventory your life and review your blueprint to ensure you are going in the right direction.

All of your thoughts so far have brought you to where you are. Yes, you do have the power to choose what you think about and what you focus your attention on. But it starts with becoming aware of exactly what you are thinking. That starts with personal reflection. Take a few moments each day to figuratively step out of your body and look at your thoughts as if they were coming from a third person. This approach will help to separate you from your personal attachments and look at your life objectively.

Try this exercise whenever you find yourself in a downward spiral or a confused maze of your thoughts. At times, we can get a worrisome or negative thought and before we know it, we have been dwelling on the same crazy thought for two hours. It is almost as if we cannot shake it. The key is to become aware that you are about to go down this crazy rabbit hole of negative thought. Shift gears immediately and become engaged in another activity. I call it "My Step Out of Myself" method. After first utilizing it and realizing it actually works for me, I have since used it many times in different types of challenging experiences and situations.

For example, in a particularly tense discussion between team members during a meeting at work, I decided to stay very quiet and observe what was happening. It turned out that by being silent and aware, I realized each engineer needed to be heard. At times, it can be difficult to agree upon certain situations and solutions. By allowing the discussion to play out and offering everyone the opportunity to be heard and say their two-cents, we all began to relax and started to focus and make progress on what we really needed to achieve at that particular time.

Stepping out of yourself can be especially helpful when your emotions tend to come into play. First, it calms you momentarily. It allows you to get re-centered and balanced so you immediately stretch your perspective of the situation. So then a situation that could have turned into a very heated argument is turned into a mutual understanding and you dodge an otherwise uncomfortable and unnecessary experience.

Next time you find yourself in a challenging interaction or circumstance, try taking a step back and simply breathe. See the situation from an outsider's perspective. That way you can come to the most levelheaded and calm decision on how you would prefer to handle the particular obstacle. Awareness is key, as the goal is for you to become a fantastic architect and master builder to ensure your life is easy, calm, and peaceful.

The Three Essentials

Think about your life for a second. There are many things that you have perfect control over, and others that no matter how hard you try to hold on to them, they will simply slip through your hands like sand. When architecting your ideal life, it is crucial to focus on the controllables, but even more specifically, three specific pieces of the puzzle.

Consider these intangible and vital pieces of your life that you have control over:

> **Thoughts you think:** Take time at the end of each day to reflect on the thoughts that went through your mind on that day. What do your thoughts look like? By taking a few moments and evaluating your thoughts, you will get clarity and a better understanding of why you are thinking what you are thinking.

> **Images you visualize.** Images are powerful. And often times, our visualizations propel us in specific directions. We think in pictures. What images make you happy? Focus on those images to ensure you maintain a positive and upbeat attitude.

> **Actions you take.** As we traverse this world, it is the action's we choose to take that ultimately define the course of our life direction. You always have a choice. What actions do you want to take today?

Make the most of them to determine the outcome of your life by implementing these controllables with the following steps:

> ➢ Whatever you can conceive, you can achieve.

> ➢ Write down this formula:
> "Imagination + Vividness + Clarity = Reality"

> ➢ Dream and imagine what you ultimately want for you. Imagine "It."

> ➢ Knowing the "It" is the key element in helping you believe that whatever it is you want can happen for you.

The best architects in the world focus on the things they can control. They do not concern themselves and focus energy on those things that they cannot change. It is vital to putting your energy in the right place. And the right place is in the compartments that you can design and redesign. You may not be able to dictate how people may behave, but you can certainly have the power to manage how you behave. Simply put, when trying to become a master builder, focus on the controllables.

Get Up!

Self-worth, the overall appraisal of your own worth, is an important factor in determining your happiness and success in many areas of your life, including your relationships and your career. When it comes to architecting and imagineering your ideal life, evaluating your self-worth and exactly how you assess your personal appeal is imperative to laying a foundation for your existence, we are all born with an innate sense of self-worth. As we move through life the events and attitudes we experience can wear down this natural sense of self-worth. But your experiences can also fortify this as well.

For Example, when I was five years old, my father took my sister and me to McDonald's for lunch. Our family very rarely went out to eat, so this was a particularly special occasion. We picked out a table and my dad said, "Siobhan, hold the table while we go order our food."

While I was sitting at the table by myself, a group of men and women approached me. One of the grown-ups told me I could not sit at the table I was holding for my family. After I explained to the stranger my father instructed me to hold the table, the man insisted that I had to move. Intimidated, I did and all five grown-ups sat down. They proceeded to unpack their burgers and fries, settling in comfortably at our table.

You can imagine how upsetting this was for me. My father told me to hold the table and I really tried, yet I felt absolutely powerless. Just at that moment, he and my sister walked up and asked me what had happened to the table? I told them the whole story.

My father immediately turned toward the people sitting at our table. I must say he was a pretty imposing figure with a build of 6'3" and a very strong presence. He then looked down at the men and women who stole our table and said, "Get up."

They responded with words of disagreement. My father leaned closer to them and repeated, "I had my daughter hold this table for us. Now get up."

I will never forget this moment. While all of this was unfolding, my little body was shaking, suspended in time, with a feeling of complete surrealism.

The group of people who were rude and disrespectful to me packed-up their food and left. They put their burgers and other items in bags, very quickly, right before my eyes. Not a single sound was uttered.

My father, standing quietly by, looked over at me and nodded his head with a little grin. I felt like I was ten feet tall. I had been vindicated. At that moment, my heart swelled with pride. My dad had stood up for me and demonstrated it right in front of my five-year-old eyes. Right then and there, unbeknownst to me, my father had appraised and reinforced my self-worth, and boy was it a wonderful feeling. I literally went from feeling like a complete failure to an undeniable success.

My Dad made me feel important that day. He showed me how much I meant to him as his little girl. That moment of complete validation from my precious dad will be etched onto my heart forever.

Self-worth is based upon our feelings of valuing ourselves. Each and every one of us is entitled to feel good about our own happiness and needs, regardless of other's judgments or opinions. It is crucial to understand your value and when architecting your ideal life, give yourself credit for all that you have accomplished, and all that you will. Let the people around you reinforce your high self-worth and use their strength to support your journey.

Your Emotional vs. Your Rational Mind

As an architect and a master builder of your life, it is important to have an emotional balance, one that you build yourself, but also one that you are comfortable in is an accurate representation of your demeanor and character.

We all know of people who are extremely emotional. At the other end of the spectrum, there are some who are immensely rational, but sometimes forget that passion and emotion are essential to finding success. Both of these types of personalities have positives and negatives. Those with an emotional mind can be loving, caring and wonderfully supportive in difficult situations, but can at times get overly involved and often times allow their passion to get the best of them. On the flip side, the more rational side mind relies on fact and logic, and can be depended upon to be levelheaded in any challenging situation. However, they may be lacking passion and can come across as emotionally detached, rarely infusing their sentiment into life.

The ideal mixture is that of the wise mind combined with a compassionate heart, thereby falling somewhere in the middle of the spectrum. It comes down to finding a balance and a happy medium, which is where the challenge lies. Marsha Linehan, an American psychologist and author, focused on the application of behavioral models combining behavioral science with concepts of mindfulness. For example, envision two circles side by side overlapping in the middle. You have the rational side on the left side of your mind, and the emotional side of the right side of your mind. Where they intersect is known as the wise mind.

Our goal is to find this intersection and develop a wise mind. It all falls back to being in balance and being mindful of what is happening at any moment. This concept helps to draw each of us in and prevent us from becoming more emotional than need be. It is also a coping mechanism, which can be used to take a step back and look at a situation with logic and reason. Finding your "wise mind" is a lifelong journey, but once you discover this equilibrium, it is a powerful tool that will help you navigate through your journey.

For example, engineers are often stereotyped as being too rational. They are all logic, and it sometimes is very difficult for them to display emotion, and demonstrate visual passion towards life. Men also can tend to be more in their rational minds. On the other hand, females can tend more toward their emotional minds. So much of it can be our nature, but being overly emotional or ridiculously regimented can present problems.

Neither type is right or wrong. It's just important to be cognizant of the spectrum of mindset approach among the people you encounter every day. It is called BMA or balanced mind awareness. As you move through life, you have to maintain a strong BMA. The intersection of your emotion and your rational thinking is a vital balance that has to be struck to lay a proper foundation for your ideal life. Your BMA is a manageable goal if you constantly assess and reassess how you are reacting to experiences and challenges in your life.

We all fall into one category more so than another. Some of us are more rational, while others are more emotional. But the most successful people in the world are the ones that evaluate where they may fall and tweak their reactions to reflect a proper BMA. The goal is to be somewhere in the middle, and strike the proper chord to create a melodious "wise mind" in decision-making and our interpersonal relationships. Then, and only then, can you take the necessary steps to begin architecting your ideal life.

Capturing the Essence of You

To architect a successful life for yourself, it is important to think creatively and outside of the box. There are many exercises you can utilize to discover unique and novel themes and notions about you that you may have never even known. Finding these undiscovered gems will help in your journey to building your fulfilling life.

I want you to get your mind thinking in a different perspective. Take a few minutes to answer the questions below. To get the proverbial ball rolling, I have provided my answers to these questions to give you some ideas. They are just a way to think outside the box. A way of seeing yourself in a different light. I've listed my answers below but first I want you to give it a try.

If you were:

➢ a beautiful piece of architecture, what would you look like?

_____

➢ a color, which color would you be?

_____

➢ a season, which season would you be?

_____

➢ a car, what type of car would you be?

_____

➢ a dog or cat, what type would you be?

_____

➢ a sport, which sport would you be?

_____

➢ a body of water, what type would you be? (ocean, lake, river)

_____

➢ if you were an animal, what type of animal would you be?

_____

➢ a piece of art, what would you be?

_____

➢ a style of music, what tempo or style would you be?

_____

➢ a flower, which flower would you be?

_____

My Responses

➢ a beautiful piece of architecture, what would you look like?
   Egyptian Pyramids (majestic, inspiring)

➢ a color, what color would you be?
   Bright Blue (vibrant, bright)

➢ a season, what season would you be?
   Summer (warm, sunny, relaxed)

➢ a car, what type of car would you be?
   Yellow Maserati (fun, fast)

➤ a dog or cat, what type would you be?
Golden Retriever (playful, loving)

➤ a sport, what sport would you be?
Kayaking (active, peaceful)

➤ a body of water, what type would you be? (ocean, lake, river)
River (fast, fresh)

➤ if you were an animal, what type of animal would you be?
Dolphin (playful, full of spirit, protective)

➤ a piece of art, what would you be?
Botticelli Angels (true, precious, kind)

➤ a style of music, what tempo or style would you be?
Classical, 80's Rock (magnificent, inspiring)

➤ a flower, what flower would you be?
Sunflower (sunshine, bright, sways in the wind)

By taking a very personal and intimate look in your heart and soul from many different angles, some concrete, and others more abstract, it will allow you the distinct opportunity to truly understand what you are made of and what you hold close to your heart. Once you understand your most fundamental makeup, you will have the ability to design and build a successful and prosperous life.

Playing Well with Others

When we understand ourselves it makes it much easier to understand others. Throughout life, you are always going to have to deal with people. Each and every day of our lives, we come into contact with all different types of people from unique and different backgrounds. Human behavior, unlike engineering, is not an exact science. It's subjective; it's open to interpretation. Human nature can be wonderful but quite challenging at times. It is not just facts. People have a range of emotions and reactions, all of which can be unpredictable and even erratic. That being said, when architecting your ideal life, it is crucial to consider your relationships with the people with which you surround yourselves.

When building a foundation for your ideal life, many things go into the make-up and fibers of this base. Your friends and family account for an enormous part of this base for your ideal life. That being said, how you interact with others will ultimately define the type of life you end up living. More than anything, both you and your friend's temperaments' will control much of the ability you will have to interrelate.

The word "temperament" is defined as: "a person's nature as it controls their behavior." Temperament is essentially a person's operating system. It is what controls the execution of their emotions. We are each "wired" a certain way. Think of it as your innate self or your nature.

The concept of temperament can be broken down into a simple and relatable four-quadrant model that will help to identify the different temperament types. Once you understand more clearly what makes people tick (including yourself), you will be better able to communicate with them and interact with greater ease, helping you effectively use their positive character to design a strong infrastructure for your own life.

First, it is necessary to identify your primary and secondary temperament type. Once you identify who you are, you will be in a better position to effectively improve and assess your temperament, all while recognizing the little quirks of each type.

The next step is identifying the different qualities for each social style and temperament type. Based on my paradigm, there are four different types of temperaments. Each one correlates to what inevitably becomes a specific type of personality. Each person will naturally fall in one of these categories, and generally speaking, project this type temperament day in and day out. Take a look at these four distinct types temperaments and consider which category you may fall in:

> ### The Architect

Determined, practical, and independent but can sometimes come across as pushy and demanding.

> ### The Builder

Enthusiastic, energetic, and friendly but can sometimes come across as impulsive and excitable.

> ### The Planner

Dependable, concerned, and empathetic but can sometimes come across as hesitant and wishy-washy.

> ### The Engineer

Analytical, persistent, and organized but can sometimes come across as critical and picky.

While most people will identify as an architect, builder, planner, or engineer regarding their temperament, others may be a mix of multiple quadrants. The objective here is to understand the other person's behavior with a different set of eyes because we are all not the same. Once you can identify the type of person you are dealing with, only then can you find common ground and balance with their personality. We all have a tendency to view other people from our own frame of reference. When you are interacting with different types of people, you have to work hard to understand why they behave and react the way do.

Obviously, most people will be a combination of all of these personality types, but do your best to assess which set of characteristics best defines them. To go in even more depth, consider the following:

The **"Architect"** is very task-oriented and their motto is "**Just do it**." When dealing with them, speed up, get to the point and provide options. Their temperament type probably gives you the impression that they know what they want, where they are going and how to get there quickly.

The "**Builder**" is very people-oriented and quick. Their motto is "**Have fun doing it**." When talking with them, speed up, sell your idea in a positive way and have fun. Their temperament type is that they are communicative, warm, approachable and competitive. They involve other people with their feelings and thoughts.

The **"Planner"** is process-oriented and people-oriented. Their motto is "**Do it together.**" When dealing with these people, slow down, lay out the plan step by step, be honest, sincere and supportive. Their temperament type places a high priority on friendships, close relationships and cooperative behavior. They get involved in feelings and relations between people.

The **"Engineer"** is very task-oriented like the architect, but process oriented as well. Their motto is "**Do it right the first time.**" When dealing with them, slow down, lay out the facts and let them speak for themselves. Their temperament type lives life according to facts, principles, logic and consistency. They are often viewed as cold and detached, but appear to be cooperative in interactions, as long as they can have freedom of choice.

The key to understanding other people is to start by understanding yourself. Once you reflect and appreciate your personality type better, it will help you better determine your ultimate life plan, and offer the opportunity to look towards others to become meaningful pieces of your blueprint.

Most of us do not take the vital time to actually understand what makes each of us tick. We walk through life and rarely do we place ourselves under a microscope and study the fibers of our being. After this personal assessment, it will provide valuable insight into your ability to grasp and appreciate other people.

Through relating and realizing the intrinsic worth in others, you will be able to channel the energy and experiences of those people and not only learn from them, but allow them to inspire you to architect a beautiful and successful life. When you begin to comprehend your personal temperament, it will make it easier to not only understand yourself, but to build strong relationships with all types of personalities and characteristics of others.

The Turtle And The Scorpion

To gain insight into others, you have to take a deep look at their nature. It defines so much of who they are and how they behave. When you are trying to architect a meaningful life around you, to pick those people that fulfill your needs, you have to understand what type of people they are and what type of nature they carry.

For example, once there was a turtle that liked to swim across the river. One day a scorpion walked up to him and said, "Hello Mr. Turtle, may I have a ride across the river?"

The turtle looked at the scorpion and said, "No, you will sting me."

The scorpion said, "No, I will not. If I did that then I would drown, too."

The turtle trustingly replied, "Okay, I will give you a ride," because that made sense to him. So the turtle gave the scorpion a ride across the river but, half way across the river, the scorpion stung the turtle. The turtle looked around and said, "I thought you said you wouldn't sting me."

The scorpion said, "I know I said that, but it is my nature."

When you can't understand why people are acting a certain way, it is vital to look at their intrinsic nature because it is their nature; their intrinsic nature. By that, I mean their firmware, the way a person is wired. Sometimes it can be very challenging dealing with certain individuals. When you understand their temperament type it may become a bit easier to interact with them at times.

Understanding people is an astounding way to help architect your own life as we consistently learn life's most precious lessons through others. We can only live one life and have a limited number of experiences through our own personal journey, but through channeling the life events of others, we have an endless amount of variety that we have encountered from which we can study.

Most people's nature defines so much of who they are. And since we all come from different walks of life with numerous life experiences, relating to people can often times be challenging. However, to be a master builder and architect a full life, you have to look onto others as you look into yourself. Finding common ground and empathizing with both people and their actions will provide vital insight into not only who they are, but also how you can build them into your blueprint.

Ponder for a Moment

To understand the type of person you are, it is imperative to reflect on the positive qualities that you possess. When building a house, an architect will always highlight the most beautiful parts of it. The same is true when building your master plan for life. You have to play to your advantages and focus your efforts on the things that you are good at and excel in.

If you think that you are smart or handsome, write that down. If you are great at something, this is the time to brag about yourself. I have listed below some of my positive qualities to give a jump-start if necessary. Make sure to put your name in front of positive qualities. Here goes.

Your positive qualities:

_____

_____

Siobhan's positive qualities:
Friendly, Out-going, Honest, Loyal, Trustworthy, Intelligent, Positive, Well-Educated, Independent, Hard-Worker, Fun-loving, Genuine, Caring, Responsible, Good-Friend

This is a challenging exercise for me and I know for many of you it will be as well. We are just not used to reinforcing the positive qualities we do possess. And we should do this more often.

Notice not just what you wrote down, but in what order those qualities are in. It is interesting to see how you think of yourself and which qualities you may value most (or at least the ones that come to mind the quickest). Also take note of whether writing any of these characteristics made you feel uncomfortable. Take a moment to think about why. Is this particular quality one with which you struggle? Or perhaps it's something other people see in you that you cannot see in yourself. Either way, the simple task of putting pen to paper can help bring to light your most innate and strong qualities.

To take this exercise even further, approach some of your close friends and ask them to write down a list of your positive qualities. Then compare their list to yours. You should notice which qualities might be missing from one list or the other. Spend some time with this warm-up because it may help you mesh your self-perception with how others see you. This exercise should give you the tools to incorporate who you are into your vision for an ideal life.

With Whom do you Surround Yourself?

In life, we always want to surround ourselves with those that uplift us, rather than bring us down. When designing your blueprint for a quality life, it is important to understand who will help to build your dream home. Would you want a bunch of lazy and negative people constructing your house? Probably not. It will be reflected in the quality of the end result. The same is true in your life. People who bring positive energy into your life will help architect a meaningful and successful life. And those that do not simply should not have a place in your life.

I have some of the most wonderful friends. The type of friends that are supportive, kind, caring, and fun. I always know I can rely on them in any situation. And I know I would be there for them in a heartbeat if needed. Friends are very important. They are the ones you can always share a laugh with and the ones who will be there for you when you need a kind word or shoulder to lean upon.

Take a moment and take inventory of your friends and whom you surround yourself with. This is important. Negative people are toxic. This behavior is infectious in a very, very bad way. Imagine a bubble as your positive energy, and imagine these negative people pricking it with a pin, literally bursting your sense of self with their negativity.

Such people often times enjoy projecting their negativity onto others. This has happened to me. I made an oath to myself that I would no longer spend time with negative people when I can avoid them. It feels just like tar being thrown over me.

In life, you have to surround yourself with positive and upbeat people. Although there are some people you cannot change, like family or co-workers, most of the people that share your journey with you will be by your own decision. You can end a friendship, but your family is always your family. Remember that. Remove yourself from any situation when it gets negative because only you have control of the people with whom you architect your life.

In life, we all have a limited amount of time. We make time for what is important, and the people who have positive energy and help nurture our gardens are those that should receive the majority of our time. Take a look around and figure out the people that help you plant the seeds, and water those seeds, and grow a beautiful garden. Those are the people who will help architect a fantastic master plan for both you and your life.

Excellence

Have you ever asked yourself why some people have extraordinary lives while others just have ordinary lives? Do you ever wonder why some people constantly reach for excellence and do the very best they can in every area of their lives? Well the simple answer is that there are a group of people in this world that when architecting their ideal life, focus on excellence and never settle for anything less. This is a special group of people and there is no reason why you cannot be a part of this elite assembly.

I know that when I call a hotel to make a reservation and get a person who answers the phone with a bland and monotonous voice, I just say, "Sorry, wrong number" and hang up. Why waste my time and energy? You can tell when people want to be exceptional and high producers in their field. For example, let's say you ask a colleague to do something simple, like sharpen a pencil, and they act as if it's just so much work. I am being a bit facetious here with this example, but I think you get my point.

The littlest things are so difficult for them to do, whereas there are other people you can ask to do something, and they're right on it. This type of individual performs the task, gets it done, and does it very well. That is the type of person I want you to be, if you are not already. You can become the epitome of excellence.

The majority of people don't go that extra ten percent or even an extra one percent. Always go the extra mile, because you will be eons ahead of the rest. Just remember, water doesn't boil at 211 degrees; water boils at 212 degrees. I want you to go that extra degree.

Architecting your ideal life, more than anything else, is about not only reaching for greatness and excellence, but also implementing it into your everyday life. It is crucial that you hold yourself to a high level and when assessing your personal goals and accomplishments, to never forget how vital that extra one-degree can be.

Ponder for a Moment

Who would you love to meet? The reason why I am asking you to think about this for a moment, is so you can reflect on who has inspired you. Who have you admired because of their exceptional achievements? Or just simply, who would be fun to meet? This is not about being star-struck either. I believe we are all stars in our own right. Each and every one of us has a gift, a unique talent that we can share and help others.

Write down 10 people you wish you could meet that are alive today.

_____

_____

_____

My list:

Ellen DeGeneres, Oprah Winfrey, George Lucas, Steven Spielberg, Maria Shriver, Sandra Bullock, Robin Williams, Ted Turner, Donald Trump, Warren Buffett

Write down 10 people you wish you could meet who have passed on.

_____

_____

_____

My list:

Leonardo Da Vinci, Albert Einstein, Joan of Arc, Walt Disney, Princess Diana, St. Francis of Assisi, Galileo Galilei, Queen Elizabeth the 1st, Ben Franklin, Charles Lindbergh

Snippets: Brain Phenomena

Right Brain vs. Left Brain

Right brain thinkers are usually more creative, emotional, intuitive, playful, spontaneous, and artistic. Left-brain thinkers are usually more rational, analytical, literal, linear, skeptical, mathematical, and cautious.

Itelligence Quotient

An intelligence quotient, or IQ, a number representing a person's reasoning ability measured using problem-solving standardized tests designed to assess intelligence. Approximately 95% of the population have an IQ score between 70 and 130. In 1956, known as one of the smartest people in the world, Marilyn vos Savant, scored 228 on an IQ test when she was just ten years old.

Incredible Minds

Sixteenth century Florence was known for having the greatest number of artists, in the same place, at any one time, in the history of our world. These incredible artists as well as neighbors to one another include: Leonardo Da Vinci, Michelangelo, Botticelli, and Raphael. DaVinci was also an architect, engineer, renowned scientist, mathematician, and painter.

Plus Up

The reason I am asking you these questions is to get you thinking and focused on what it is you actually do want in life. Consider these questions and the role they may play in your life:

➤ What natural gifts and strengths do you possess?

➤ What comes easily to you?

➤ What is most important to you?

➤ If you could accomplish just three things in your life, what would they be?

➤ Who, as the architect, do you surround yourself with?

➤ What type of person are you, what is your temperament?

➤ Are you a doer or a thinker?

➤ Do you live in the present, past, or future?

➤ What would your closest friends or family write about you in one paragraph?

➤ If you could make just one change in your life, what would it be?

5

The Site
EYE ON PARADISE

"The real voyage of discovery consists not in seeking new landscapes, but in having new eyes."

—MARCEL PROUST

Finding Balance in Paradise

Throughout the preceding chapters, we have spent time discussing your innate ability to create a blueprint for your ideal life. We then spoke about how to implement this plan into your life and the meaningful ways you can begin to build and architect what you want and desire for your future. But now it is time to begin to focus on where this ideal life is going to occur and how you are going to balance all the moving pieces of your life. Are you going to build a life centered on family? Or friends? Or work? Or philanthropy? How are these parts of your schematic going to interplay and relate to one another? That is the crux of this chapter.

The idea of keeping your eyes on paradise falls on the fundamental notion that you have to decide where you will make your vision a reality, and how you will balance this reality within your personal paradise. Life is like a meticulously hand built watch. There are millions of moving pieces and when placed together in the appropriate manner, they will work together and the result will be a fully functional and working wristwatch. However, if one part is missing or unbalanced, the watch will not work. The same is true in life. You have to find the pieces of your life and balance them with one another to ensure that your life functions. If you do not do that, you will just have a series of parts with no movement.

When I was finishing Architecture school, I was desperately seeking employment. I received an interesting job offer from a company in Idaho. However, I frequently visited my sister on weekends in San Diego while I was attending Arizona State University. I fell in love with the beauty of the city and I knew in my heart that is where I was meant to live.

Even though I had yet to find a job in San Diego, I just could not imagine moving to Idaho because I had envisioned my life in San Diego. My eyes were on paradise, and that paradise was on the West Coast. I had my clear vision of where I wanted to build this ultimate life. And then once I got the job, I had to balance the equilibrium and find a sense of personal stability. If you have a clear blueprint, and are ready to architect your ideal life, but cannot find steadiness or poise, you will never reach your goals and your paradise.

What You Surround Yourself With

Before we can begin finding the location for your paradise and balancing your new life, it will be helpful to inventory exactly what is going on in your current life. You can improve only what you assess. Consider the following questions before we begin searching for a balanced paradise:

➢ What does your life look like?

➢ Are you happy, peaceful and content?

➢ Do you look forward to and embrace each day?

➢ Do you want to lead an ordinary or an extraordinary life?

I know that if you picked up this book, you want to lead an extraordinary life. I guarantee I know you can. We just need to do a little inventory first.

➢ How is your health?

➢ How is your weight, appearance, etc.?

➢ How do you feel? Could things be better?

➢ What is your state of mind? Are you usually happy or unhappy?

➢ Are you the "glass is half full" type of person or the "glass is half empty" type of person?

➢ What is your home environment like? Are you Pigpen, like the Peanuts character? Or is your home organized, clean, fresh and bright? Is your home a happy serene place where you can hang your hat and relax?

➢ What are your relationships like?

➢ Are you and your significant other loving, caring, supportive and happy together?

> ➤ Are your friendships strong enough to support you in times of adversity? And in celebrations?

> ➤ Do you reciprocate your strength, love, and support to friends in need?

Answering these questions should help you accurately assess if you live a balanced and full life, or if you need to spend time considering how you move the pieces around so that you have a strong equilibrium.

The Balance of Friends and Family

We all want and need friends. As you traverse your life, friendships will prove to be one of the most special parts of the journey. The people we meet and with which we interact will shape who we become. Balancing your friendships is not only a skill, but also a resource you will use to help imagineer your ideal life. There are only so many minutes in the day. It is respectful to allot your time in a balanced manner to your friends and family.

The people that love you will want to spend time with you and become integral parts of your life. I have found it can be a great challenge to give these friendships the time they deserve. But when it comes down to it, they are the ones who will be there for us when we are taking our many walks through life. Through trials and tribulations, hard times and good times, your friendships are precious.

With whom you surround yourself has a deep impact on who you ultimately become. This is one of the areas in your life that you have the power to change. *You may not need to make huge changes, just a small modification here or there can make an enormous difference, ultimately creating enormous shifts in your life.* To find the correct balance between friends and family, start by considering who your closest friends and family members are.

An easy way to come to this consideration is by asking yourself, "if something great or something terrible happened to me, who would I call first to celebrate or for support?" The people that immediately come to mind are those that are closest to you and your life. Now it is time to consider the amount of time you give to those friends and family members. Often times in life, the people who we would call first in sickness and in health are not the people that we invest the majority of our time with. These are the difference makers in your life and through this simple assessment, you can come to terms with the schematics you implement into your own life.

It is also crucial in your life to think about the type of people that will help propel you to paradise. You constantly have to be looking forward, trying to establish a location for your future life, and my goal is to help you find one that you consider the perfect location, both literally and figuratively speaking. Your friends and family will inevitably become the people that surround you on this metaphorical island. Think about those people that will inspire you, motivate you, and elevate your life. Those are the people that will help you navigate the torrential seas and find your dream life.

> *"Be the change you want to see in the world."*
>
> —MAHATMA GANDHI

Finding Paradise

Finding the perfect place for your paradise may seem like a daunting task. But it does not have to be. In reality, it really comes down to taking your vision and letting it guide you to where you want to be in life. Whether we are talking about a literal location to reside, or even a vision for the future, keep your eyes on your idea of paradise and let your journey lead you to it.

Let me tell you a story about Art and Walt. These two friends go way back. Walt had just bought some land and called Art to say, "Hey friend, you have to think of buying the land adjacent to the land that I just invested in. It will be worth a fortune one day, I guarantee it." Art was already well off, owned a lot of real estate and replied, "I just don't see it worth the investment." Art hesitated for a moment and declared, "No, I have decided not to invest."

It turned out Walt was Walt Disney and Art was Art Linkletter, very well known for the 1950's television show, "Kids Say the Darndest Things." At that time Walt Disney had a vision of building theme parks for wonderful happy family entertainment. For each and every one of us, it all begins with a vision. Walt had just begun his vision and had just begun building Disneyland in Anaheim, California. His paradise was California, and he was destined to turn his vision into a reality.

Incredible story. Illustrating the point of how we all make our own choices and how our choices are implicit to each and every one of our outcomes. Looking toward your paradise will help to guide you to create the life you desire. Sometimes, it is okay that the choice you once made was not exactly the best decision at the time. Always know you have control of the choices you make.

A Cold Jersey Night

Envisioning your own paradise can start at a very young age. It does not have to be convoluted or overly involved. It can simply be your desire to be somewhere else. The point is that we are greatly affected by our surroundings. The thought of waking up each and every day to cold and muggy weather was never for me. Some people enjoy the snow and layering before they walk out of the door, but I am more of a sunny kind of gal. When I was eleven years old we moved to a beautiful small town just north of the New York City named Tenafly, New Jersey. My Mom chose Tenafly because of its exceptional school system. She and my Dad always told us the importance of a good education, so they did all that they could to make sure that was available for my sister and me.

It was a wonderful idyllic town and I loved growing up there. I also made some of the best friends that are still in my life today. Growing up was a lot of fun. It was your typical all-American small town, with football games, Friday night bonfires, dates with boys, and sleepovers with my best girlfriends. It was wonderful and at times challenging going through the typical teenager's life. But I feel so incredibly blessed to have had that type of experience.

Fast-forward eight years. I was nineteen and home from college in Boston. I was studying Mechanical Engineering at Northeastern University. My sister, Dawn and I shared a bedroom. She was living at home, working as a Pharmacist at the local town pharmacy.

It was a bitter cold Jersey night and we were tucked in our beds all warm and safe under our down comforters. We had on long flannel dress pajamas, and we could hear the biting wind howling outside and cold rain was pounding the windows. I loved that bedroom which we had really fixed up to be a truly wonderful warm fun room.

My sister, Dawn and I were talking and whispering across that late very cold Jersey night. She starts to say, "Do we really want to live in this type of weather?" She goes on to say, "What are we just going to eat bonbons and stay inside all the time or we can move to California?" We made a pact that cold winter North Jersey night that each of us would move out west someday, somehow. I have now been living in San Diego for over twenty-years and my sister has as well. Thank you God for that cold North Jersey night.

Assessing your life and finding out what type of place makes you happy is crucial to creating a satisfying existence. Our surroundings dictate so much of our attitude and mood. Life is challenging enough without challenges that we create. We do not have control over many experiences that we may have, but the basic decision of where our paradise falls is one decision that we can control. That being said, putting yourself in a place that makes you fundamentally unhappy is an unnecessary hurdle.

Consider your non-negotiables. That is, the facets of your ideal paradise that you simply will not give up. Perhaps you have to be close to water. Or you may want to be in a major metropolitan city, or in a quiet neighborhood, or maybe far away from brutal winters. Whatever it may be, it is your responsibility to shape your life with these choices in mind.

Balancing Paradise

In life, it is vital to find balance. Balance amongst the people you love, balance amongst your work and personal life, balance amongst when you focus and when you relax, and balance amongst finances, time, and responsibilities. If you cannot find balance, you will always feel like your life is falling short. Do you ever take the time to slow down? Are you always rushing, going from here to there trying to finish all your lists, check-check-check? Remember the saying, "When you die, your inbox is still going to be full."

With the hectic pace we all have become used to these days, it's no wonder why we feel so over-worked and stressed-out. Each and every day seems like just another day in the rat race. It is as if there is just not enough time to get everything that you need and want to get done in the day. So you have no choice but to prioritize and find balance in your personal paradise because if you do not, paradise will be no more.

So as you navigate your journey, here are some helpful ways to find a more balanced life:

Take Time to Relax. We all have our ways to unwind and kick back. For example, mediation is a refreshing and unique way to recharge. Meditation quiets and relaxes the mind. The definition of meditation is being in a state of extreme relaxation and concentration, in which the mind is quieted of thought and the body is at rest. It's how you can get in touch with your inner self. It is incredibly important to take some quiet time for you each day.

In actuality, meditation calms and focuses your mind. It is a bit of a paradox. A self-contradiction, making us ask the question, "How can slowing down and becoming centered help me? Because I have so much to do, now!"

To practice meditation, simply sit in a quiet place for five to ten minutes. With your eyes closed, focusing on your breathing. Letting all thoughts just pass on by. Being still and in the very present moment. All is quiet for those few moments. You should be at peace. This is an opportunity to reflect and take time away from the difficult challenges life can often present. Meditation is just one example of ways you can relax. There are many more. Perhaps it is a massage, trip to the gym, reading a good book, watching a movie, and walking your dog, or anything and everything in between. The point is that you have to find your coping mechanism and your way to recharge and implement it into your life.

Turn off Your Mind. Have you ever tossed and turned in bed, unable to go to sleep because you were so focused and engaged on something? Often times, we spend much of our time with our mind in thought and focused on what is happening in life. It is crucial to take time and simply turn off your mind. Whether you prefer to read a book, watch a movie, or simply take a nap, you should find time each and every day to give your mind some rest time. Let it relax and recharge. Your mind is a powerful tool, but with training, it needs time to recover. If not, you will find you are tired and worn out, both of which will affect your ability to perform in your life, both professionally and personally.

Take Care of your Body. How you feel will often times reflect in how you act. If you are healthy and your body is strong, you will be able to easily navigate life. But without your health, you will find that you are lethargic, unable to accomplish goals quickly and efficiently, and spend time recovering rather than doing. We only have one body and often times we do not take care of our most prized possession. Eating right, working out, and most importantly, balancing your internal needs will help to create a healthy body, which will inevitably create a healthy mind.

Eyes on Paradise

As you imagineer your ideal life, you will find that your paradise can come in many different shapes and sizes. Everyone is different and each of us desires our own version of paradise. It can be location, lifestyle, or the people with which we surround ourselves. Paradise is not only about the who, what, and where, but also concerns how each of us balances those elements.

For example, even the richest man in the world probably wants more. More time with his family, more time with his friends, more visits to the gym, more occasions to relax, and more balance in his life. It does not matter who you are. Each of us can tweak and change our ideal life. It starts with a personal assessment, understanding exactly how the pieces of your life interact with one another.

Paradise is reachable. It does not have to feel like some distant concept that you will never come close to finding. We all make our personal paradise with every decision and action we make. The job we take, the family we love, the friends we spend time with, and the location we call home all have considerable effects on our ability to build our paradise.

Think about what makes you happy, what makes you tick, and consider the type of life you want to live. Find the surroundings that give you a pleasant and warm feeling inside to light your soul on fire. Keep your eye on paradise and take steps every waking moment of your life to reach your goals and find your perfect personal paradise.

Snippets: A Beautiful Site

The New World

Christopher Columbus (1452-1506), the European explorer discovered America in 1492. The indigenous people in North America were composed of distinct tribes and ethnic groups, who in fact had been living in America for close to 20,000 years before Columbus. The name for these people became known as "Indians" which originated from Columbus who thought he had landed in the East Indies.

Three Hundred Islands

The largest group of artificial islands, called "The World," has been created off the coast of Dubai. Measuring 5.5 miles (9km), the islands are grouped together forming a map of the world. Sheikh Mohammed bin Rashid al Maktoum, the ruler of Dubai was the visionary and creator of such a site.

Building Up into the Sky

The concept of building high still is amazing if you have ever watched a skyscraper being built. In the late 19th century, Architects worked out how to support buildings using a steel frame which allowed really tall buildings to be constructed for the first time. Buildings made out of stone are unable to support their own weight and topple over if built higher than 500 ft (152m). So the invention of the steel frame created an abundance of new building opportunities.

Plus Up

➤ What is your job like? Is it your passion and if not, then what is?

➤ What is your perfect job, career; where do you spend your hours each day?

➤ How do you spend your personal time? Happy social events, clubs, outings, peaceful interludes, reading, and relaxing, etc.

➤ What shape are your finances in? Are you at peace with the financial path you are on?

➤ Are you thinking about what you'll need financially to retire in the lifestyle in which you imagine?

➤ Are all your financial needs met? If not, what steps can you take today to move toward that?

➤ Where is this fabulous life you are going to create?

➤ If you could live anywhere in the world, where would it be?

➤ What if money was no object? How would you choose to live your life?

➤ Who are you with at this dream location, in your paradise?

➤ What would be the most favorite part of your day?

➤ At the end of the day when you are tucking yourself in, what are you most happy about?

➤ Do you ever take a moment to envision the place you would ultimately like to spend your time? Do it now.

➤ Imagine being in that ultimate place you want to be right now. What changes need to be made for you to move closer to that place and to make it happen?

6

The Timeline
JUST NOW

*"We all must take some quiet time just for ourselves.
Time to reflect on all that has led us to this moment.
Time to dream of all the places we might go from here."*

—LOUIS CONRAD HILL

Just Now

The concept of 'Just Now' may seem foreign to most of us, as it is not a commonly used term, but that is not the case in other parts of the world. When visiting my family in Durban South Africa at the ripe age of eleven, my family and I were at a pool party, and I was with my cousin, Catherine, at her friend's home. I was a very athletic kid and excitedly said to my cousin, "Cath, let's go swim." She responded by saying, "Just now."

Well the phrase "Just Now" which I did not know at the time, means "in a little while" in South Africa. Very different from in the United States where <u>now</u> is meant as <u>right now</u>. I figured the whole thing out pretty quickly though. I relaxed and patiently waited. Cath and I did eventually swim.

While South African in origin, the phrase "Just Now" has some polarizing and important meaning when it comes to Imagineering your life's goals. Too may times in life, we focus so much on the right now that we forget about the "just now." It is not only impossible, but also unhealthy to think you can change your life overnight.

All great accomplishments take time and sometimes it's easy to get so very frustrated that what we want in life is not happening immediately and right now. Success will come if you lay the proper foundation for it. It will happen in time when you set in your mind's eye on what you truly desire. Try saying to yourself "Just Now" instead of right now in the hopes of putting yourself on a healthy and realistic timeline for your desired outcomes.

"When wise man in rush he sits down."

—UNKNOWN

The Importance of Planning

If you first do not know where you are going, you cannot conceptualize a plan. There lies the value in planning. Plotting a course before you set sail will be vital to not only how you will reach your destination, but if you will reach it at all. You have to first have a clear concise vision of your destination. The only way to achieve this clarity is thorough proper planning and forethought. Only then can you anticipate obstacles, and navigate your way to success.

The great part about imagineering your ideal life is that you are your captain, shipmates, and crew. You have control over all aspects and facets of how the ship sails. From the direction of the sails to how high they are raised to the position of the crew to operating the helm, when you imagineer your life, you call the shots. That being said, when things go right, you have no one to pat on your back but yourself, and when things go wrong, you are responsible. That is a vital part of finding personal success and growth. To plan effectively, you have to be accountable. You have to take responsibility for your choices, both good and bad, and hold yourself and your life-plan to an extremely high standard.

Imagine the most successful and fun course you could possibly take to get to your ultimate destination. It can and will be anything you want it to be. It is a white canvas to an artist, a blank sheet of paper to an architect or writer, a fresh navigation chart to a sea captain, an empty sheet of music to a composer and so on.

It all starts here and it all starts with meticulous and dedicated planning. Remain accountable, stay the course, and let your passion become your vision. You are the creator of your destiny, and you are the architect of your timeline.

> *"Yesterday is gone. Tomorrow has not yet come. We only have today. Let us begin."*
>
> —MOTHER TERESA

If you Fail to Plan, you Plan to Fail

Have you ever wondered when your best life is going to happen? Well, it's going to start happening right now if it hasn't already. Your "just now" is closer than you think. It all starts with proper planning and putting the pieces in place to reach your goals. In order to accomplish this, you need to have a strategy, goals, and milestones. Simply put, you have to prepare your timeline. Most people spend more time designing a vacation than they do designing their lives. I know how very important it is to plan out where you ultimately want to be and do in life.

There are two steps that you can take to creating a timeline and preparing for your future goals and aspirations.

The first step is to write down your succinct and specific goals that you would like to reach in the future. A list of these goals would suffice. Next, begin to summarize how long you feel it should take to reach these goals in your life. Some goals are attainable within a few days or weeks, while others may take years. Put a number next to each of your goals so you can better understand what your timeframe looks like.

The next step is to break your plan down into manageable chunks such as work, family, friends, and anything and everything in between. The most effective way I have been able to do this is to have brainstorming sessions. This is done by just letting your mind flow, not thinking about your answers, and just writing down what comes to mind. If you categorize your goals and brainstorm for each topic, you will guide your mind in the right direction. For example, let's say I am trying to improve the area of my life concerning my health. Label a piece of paper with the word "health" on top and then begin brainstorming ideas under this concept. Some ideas that may come to mind could be: workout more, eat healthy, walk the dog, spend more time outside, etc…The list can go on and on, but the activity, in and of itself, will help for you to comprehend how to reach your goals.

Furthermore, when creating a timeline, remember that it is vital to your success to create a timeline that is realistic and believable. How do you want to do it? When do you want to do it? When do you want to take breaks? Remember, you don't have to get this all done by next week.

Like designing and building a skyscraper, you must plan it out and break it into manageable milestones and parts. It takes thoughtful planning and room for delays and missteps.

You also don't want to create an unrealistic timeline.

In thinking about your timeline, account for all the responsibilities you have in your life. Each of these responsibilities will have a profound effect upon your timetable and ability to meet your personal deadlines. If your goal is to give more time to charity, you obviously would have to consider how many hours per week you work. A retired individual would be able to give more hours than someone working fifty-hour weeks. If you have a full-time job, or a house and family to tend to, then you need to figure out "*when*" during a normal week will you make time to further your life plan.

Also, like many good wines, some things in life need to breathe. It may be even better if you move at a slow but steady pace so that you have time to process what you are doing, and to consider each step of the plan carefully. Taking this time to breathe and reflect will also offer you insight into your timeline and your journey. This is a process that cannot be rushed and it takes time, dedication, and determination. But also try not to move too slowly, as you need to see progress to keep yourself motivated and moving forward. If you move slowly through your life-plan, you may find yourself procrastinating and not pushing yourself towards your goals.

> *"After all… tomorrow is another day."*
>
> —SCARLET O'HARA, *Gone With the Wind*

The Time is Now

When it comes to engineering solutions and building timelines, it is vital to your success to be clear and envision what needs to be built. That is where the concept of proper planning comes into play. When you plan, you create reachable and attainable personal goals. But the next step in building your timeline is just as important. That is, after you plan out your timetable, you have to begin taking the steps to implement your timeline into your own life. And those steps start with implementing the timeline you created.

We spoke earlier in this chapter about the "just now", which is important to maintaining your patience and pushing you forward with drive and determination. But on the same note, we have to also remember there is no time like the present and it is imperative to do what I refer to as "determined implementation." That is, move forward with your life-plan with a basic understanding that while it takes time to change and improve, every day is an opportunity to get one day closer to your goals.

One day, my twelve-year-old nephew, Grant, told me he was going to become an Eagle Scout, the highest award you can earn in the Boy Scouts of America. I was so proud of him, but do you know what it takes to become an Eagle Scout? You have to earn a total of 21 Merit badges, including some of the following: First Aid, Citizenship in the Community/Nation/World, Personal Fitness, Emergency Preparedness/Lifesaving, Swimming/Hiking/Cycling, Camping, and Family Life. Becoming an Eagle Scout takes an incredible amount of work, focus, and determination. I have always told Grant that while it may take some time to achieve his goals, before he can get fifteen, twenty, or even twenty-one merit badges, he has to start today and he has to start with the first one. The same is true in life and any daunting task, especially planning and implementing a successful life.

Days become weeks and weeks become months and months become years, and it is the years that change your life and move you closer to success. But there are 365 opportunities in each year to take 1/365th of a step closer to reaching your life's goals.

Start changing your life today by planning for your future and implementing these plans into your every day life. If losing weight is your goal, start dieting and hitting the gym today. If running a marathon is your goal, start with a couple of miles today. If building a beautiful family is your life desire, join a dating site today. We can always find an excuse to table our timeline for our lives, but a day not used is a day wasted. The time is now, otherwise how will you turn your days into years and your years into the life that you have always wished to have lived?

"If one advances confidently in the direction of one's dreams, and endeavors to live the life which one has imagined, one will meet with a success unexpected in common hours. "

—HENRY DAVID THOREAU

Building Your Plan: Brainstorming

So the question remains: How can you build a useful and effective plan to implement into your own life? Here is a list of suggestions to help you focus and make this monumental task more approachable:

- ➢ You need a time limit so as to keep you focused and prevent your mind from wandering off on tangents. I recommend you start with five minutes.

- ➢ You also need a mind that is open to every possibility, as that will provide you the greatest amount of clarity and value from this exercise.

> ➤ Absolutely no "analysis paralysis" allowed. ("Analysis paralysis" means over-thinking a situation or problem so that a decision/ action is not taken, ultimately paralyzing the outcome.)

> ➤ You must write down every idea that pops into your head.

> ➤ You can only ask one question over and over during this brainstorming session.

> ➤ Have fun. You're not being tested. This is simply getting your creative juices flowing without the logic part of your brain getting in the way.

> ➤ Your goal is to write a minimum of ten answers to the question of what you need to plan and how you're going to get it done.

This is just an exercise to get moving in the right direction and begin planning and heading where you want to go. At times it is easy to get stuck in our thinking. This may be of help when you find yourself in such a place.

Examples of Goals

Consider examples of some of the goals you may want to reach during your planning sessions. These are just a few examples, and there are many more. It will almost certainly be different for each person and the real value is finding exactly what your goals may be and how you can reach them.

Take a look at these examples to get your creative juices flowing:

> ➤ Be surrounded with wonderful family and friends

> ➤ Write a bestselling book

➢ Be happy, healthy, lean, slender, and toned

➢ Be financially free

Furthermore, take a look at an example of how to answer your timeline questions. Let's pretend for a moment that a small timeline goal is to create a fully functional, operational website. An example question could be, "How do I get my website created, and operational? "

Some answers to this question may include:

➢ Get domain name

➢ Take class on web development

➢ Look at other websites

➢ Investigate other websites I like

➢ Decide the message I want to convey

➢ Think about how I want to organize the website

➢ Figure out who the audience will be

➢ Find out how to set up e-mail on the site

> *"Map out your future but do it in pencil.*
> *The road ahead is as long as you make it.*
> *Make it worth the trip. "*
>
> —JON BON JOVI

Wow! What an exercise. Can you see it? You can create many fresh ideas when you brainstorm and are focused on your outcome. This brainstorming exercise should help you springboard into the planning stage and propel your creativity to build a timetable for the rest of your life.

*"We can do anything we want to
if we stick to it long enough."*

—Helen Keller

The next step is to sort through your list of answers that are now, effectively, your "to do" list and place them in order of importance (or perhaps in chronological order). You now have what are called milestones in your plan. These are the big goals for which you are striving. Take a big sheet of paper, place it horizontally and put a long line across the middle of it. Now put today's date at the beginning of the line and put the date six months from now at the end of the line. Write down the goal you want to achieve at the end of six months. Now break it down into one-month increments and what you can achieve each month to get closer to your goal.

This is what is done in engineering. In a very simplified version, we envision what we are going to build, create a realistic timeline to actually design and build the system and then break it down into manageable milestones. Tasks are listed under each milestone in order to successfully design and build the system first envisioned. It is a very methodical approach for developing successful solutions.

This concept can easily be employed into your own timetable. Some of your goals may be reachable in months, while others may take years to attain. Regardless, the focus of this systematic approach is to maintain a precise and orderly understanding and vision of your future aspirations and goals.

Looking Back at the Summit of Success

As you create your timeline and journey, it is vital to take time to not only focus on your journey, but also the accomplishments you have reached, the pinnacles you have scaled, and the obstacles you have overcome. Consider this example from my childhood of my first ski trip with my father.

At nineteen, I took my dad skiing. I signed him up for his first lesson while I cruised up the mountain on the chair lift. After a couple of runs, I checked on my dad and saw that he was doing great, his lesson was going well. About ninety minutes into the two-hour lesson, I checked on my dad again. From afar I could see him standing on his skis on the bunny hill surrounded by a group of children, with a complete look of boredom on his face.

I had to rescue my poor dad. I raced over and skied up to him and exclaimed, "Let's get out of here Daddy." Being the fun adventurous spirit, I asked him if he wanted to go up in the chairlift and he gave me a big smile, exasperatingly shouting, "YES!" The look on his happy face was priceless. He had been saved. We lumbered over to the lift on our skis, big smiles on our faces, cheeks red and completely windblown. We looked behind us to see the vast mountain going forever. As we travelled higher and higher into the snow-clad mountains, I began to come to terms with the reality that in just a few moments, my father, a novice skier, would have to navigate one of the most difficult parts to learn when it comes to skiing—getting off of the chairlift.

In a split second, I was now really worried. My father stands at 6'3", two long sticks attached to his feet and just learning how to ski two hours ago, any type of fall would not be pretty. What was I thinking? I knew we were headed for disaster. I lifted the bar as soon as we hit the landing point. I slid off the lift and turned around to help my father. Luckily, the ski shack guy came jumping out to help and with our arms outstretched, we pulled my father towards us, getting him safely out of the way of the other chairlifts.

As I was trying to balance him, my dad grabbed onto me, like this crazy Frankenstein and we both went flying into the snow. We managed to get rearranged as best we could and started on our way down the ski path from the infamous chairlift, to the top of the ski run. Trees surrounded us as we made our way and up ahead we saw a clearing. My dad was doing amazingly well for his first time, picking it up very quickly.

We skied the level path to the vast open clearing of the ski run and all I could hear behind me was a very definite "Jeeesssus!!!" It was none other than my dad. The run was steep. Looking back, from bunny hill to intermediate run in two hours, I have to give him so much credit. Giving the utmost encouragement, I cheered him on saying, "You can do this. I'll guide you every step of the way." I'd go forward ten feet and he would ski to me. Then I would go another ten feet and he would ski up to me again. I will never forget the smile on my father's face the whole time, and he fell down only once. When we got down to a level part where we could catch our breaths, I turned back to look at where we had just come down from.

I said, "Daddy, look back."

He turned around and looked back. He was absolutely astonished how far he had just skied down that huge mountain. I could feel and see the pride that surged in his chest. It was absolutely, for lack of but any other word, Terrific! On the mountain that day, we both stood with our hearts bursting, mine with pride and happiness and my father's, with the wonderful knowing that he had done it.

Often times in life, we do not take the time we should to look behind us and embrace the pinnacles that we scaled. We are so obsessed with reaching a goal and overcoming an obstacle that we rarely take the rewarding opportunity to marinate in and celebrate our achievements. The few moments my father and I took at the bottom of the mountain to truly comprehend what he had just accomplished has stayed with me forever. Following your timetable is great, but once you reach one of your goals, put your skis down, take off your goggles, and look over your shoulder, embracing the inspiring view of the peak that you conquered. These moments are the gold standard to drive your engine to success.

> *"Live as if you were to die tomorrow; Learn as if you were meant to live forever."*
>
> —MAHATMA GANDHI

Achieve, But Relieve

So many of us define our success by our achievements, but rarely take the time to simply relax and focus a little less on achieving and a little more on relieving. That is, relieving the stress, the trials, the tribulations, and the fast pace that life often seems to travel. We work at warp speed and sometimes we move through our timelines so quickly, crossing out achievements, but rarely celebrating them and rewarding ourselves for reaching them. Everyone has heard the story of the man that never stopped. He went on and on and on and eventually he looked back at his life, only to find that he never celebrated his success, never reflected on his accomplishments, and never worked to reduce his stress and simply relax.

Throughout this book, we have talked about many different techniques to reshape and remold your life, and one of the most undervalued skills to achieving great heights is to take time for yourself and enjoy life. Take time each day to focus on those things that make you smile, make you happy, and those that have meaning. It may be as simple as lying on the floor with your dog and letting him lick your face. When we focus all of our energy on achieving, we can often lose sight of the fruits of our labor.

I know those of you reading this book are high achievers who sometimes just don't give yourselves a break. That is why it is important to take breaks, take a walk, and take a nap. You have to enjoy life and have fun along the way. If I gave you two choices, which one would you take…Choice 1 allows you to live a life where you succeed. You reach every one of your goals with 100% certainty. But at the same time, you are just not having fun. You are overworked, focused on the wrong parts of life, and never take time for yourself. Choice 2 allows you reach most, but not all of your goals. You take time to love, to live, and to smile. You are successful in your own mind and you know you may have not reached every pinnacle but you have certainly scaled some of the taller ones in the world.

Which choice seems more attractive to you? Give yourself the time you need to enjoy all that life has to offer. Achieve but also relieve yourself of the stress life will almost certainly infuse into your life. That way, you can honestly say you have imagineered a fantastic life for yourself.

Another concept here is gestation. Everything has a period of gestation. The old saying goes, "Nine women can't make a baby in one month." Sometimes it is expected that you have to get things done when it seems utterly impossible because it takes time and you don't have the time to wait. Just like when you plant a seed and wait for it to sprout into a flower or a tree; it takes time.

Time and time again, I have seen programs that don't do this. Imagine constructing a building without a blueprint or developing a computer software system without a design. The same applies to your own life. You must strategize and design it. Begin taking steps toward achieving your goals and dreams. Now.

"You miss 100% of the shots you don't take."

—Wayne Gretzky

Just Swing the Bat

In life, sometimes you just have to clinch the bat, dig in, and take a home-run cut at the game of life. This chapter has focused on the importance of building a timeline for your life. It centers on the idea that to prepare for a great life, you have to plan for a great life. But at the same time, you have to remember that preparation without action is just as bad as not acting at all. You simply have to swing the bat.

My dad used to tell me, just swing the bat and let go of the result. Sometimes we get so caught up and worried about the results that we actually talk ourselves out of taking action. Living life comes down to keeping a fresh perspective. Sometimes we can be our own worst enemy worrying more about the destination than the journey. The purpose to creating a timeline for your life is so you can keep your eye on the prize, and remain concentrated on the end result. The point is to use our imaginations to visualize incredible and positive outcomes.

After imagineering a timeline for your future aspirations, you should have the ability to reflect much easier on your daily activities. With this reflection, you will be better positioned to learn from your timeline and pull the most out of your journey. We all want to improve and heighten our aptitude in the classroom of life. And one of the most essential pieces to this puzzle is the balance of the "just now" and the "right now." It is about manufacturing a timetable for your life, but approaching it with a stability and poise between patience ("just now") and determination ("right now"). You have this ability and with the lessons presented in this chapter, you will have all you need to create a fantastic timeline for your goals and desires.

Snippets: All in Time

Journey to the Center of Earth

The deepest part of the Earth is 1,512 miles (2,433km) deep. The center of the earth is like a magnet, a solid that contains both iron and nickel. This solid is about the size of our moon. This magnet generates a magnetic field that protects the earth from flying into orbit.

First Flight into the Sky

On December 17, 1903 the first flight into the sky occurred. The Wright brothers, Orville and Wilbur, proved flying was actually possible. The flight went up 120 ft (36.5km) and lasted only 12 seconds. This may seem insignificant in this modern age, but the billion dollar Aerospace Industry, as we know it today was born on that day in history.

First Global Positioning System

The forerunner of the first Global Positioning System (GPS) actually were the stars up in the sky. For centuries, sailors had used the moon, sun, and stars to help them navigate their ships. In 1837, Thomas Hubbard Sumner, a U.S. sea captain discovered how to use the stars to navigate the seas by plotting latitude and longitude at the same time, giving the exact position of a boat to sail the seas. It was the very beginning of faster time travel. Today the GPS is a space-based satellite navigation system used to provide location.

Plus Up

> ➢ When is this action on your plan going to happen?

> ➢ What is your action plan?

➢ Is it realistic?

➢ Is it believable?

➢ Now break your plan down into manageable milestones.

➢ List one to three actions/things you can take to reach each milestone.

➢ How will you deal with possible roadblocks?

➢ How will you handle outcomes that are out of your control?

➢ How can you better manage stress?

➢ Remember: "Event + Response = Outcome."

➢ What are your events and most importantly your responses?

➢ What are your desired outcomes?

➢ It is all up to you when you want this fabulous life to happen. When do you want to take action?

7
The Action
NOW, GO BUILD IT

*"That's one small step for a man,
one giant leap for mankind."*

—NEIL ARMSTRONG

The Power of Action

As we work hard to achieve goals and reinvent our lives, implementing lessons we have learned along the way, it is imperative to your success to never forget that at the end of the day, life is a series of actions waiting to happen. Every experience we have, every book we read, every learning opportunity that flashes in big bright lights across our eyes, is merely practice for our future actions, decisions, and journey.

With action, anything is possible. With inaction, nothing is probable. Life will uneventfully pass you by in a series of blurry images and lost prospects. Regret and remorse will fill your heart and your soul will be stuck on the "what if" forever. That is the harsh reality of not acting.

Throughout the proceeding chapters, we have discussed many different lessons you can implement into your life to build a bountiful and delightful future. Planning your life, blueprinting your goals, building a foundation. But all these are for nothing if you do not act. This chapter is about action and the value of grabbing life by the horns and never letting go.

Decisions

The crux of action is making decisions. Should you go for it or take a more conservative approach? Is this the right opportunity for you or should you wait on another one to come? Should you turn left or go right? So many times we find ourselves forgetting to act because we are paralyzed by the fundamental decision in front of us. Decisions are the basis for your actions, and being unable to make a decision is often times even worse than making the wrong decision in the first place.

In life, more times than not, we have to make difficult decisions. We have to sacrifice, risk, and even jump head first into what could be a shallow pool. It can certainly get scary out there. But making decisions is part of life and it is essential to your ability to implement your timeline to act and make a decision.

I can remember one of the toughest decisions I had to make like it was yesterday. I had finished a project six months prior and was slated to work on a new program, but we had not received funding for it yet. It was a bit of an unknown if we would get the funding or not, but I was ready to stay with my company as I really enjoyed the previous job, However, the program manager from the prior project asked me if I could deploy the same system to London.

At the time, I was reading a book, *10 Secrets of Success and Inner Peace by Wayne Dyer,* another wonderful teacher of mine. One of the chapters is "Don't Let Your Music Die Within You." I took lessons from this book to help make what seemed like a very difficult decision at the time. In my heart and soul I knew I wanted to go to London. Not only do I enjoy the work, but I wanted to go to London! Come on, who wouldn't? You don't often get an opportunity to spend four paid weeks working in England. But I was still scared that I would lose the new position I had been offered on a contract we still had yet to be awarded.

I went back the next day and despite my fears, I courageously said, "I have decided to accept the position to go to London." I made a tough decision, knowing if there was a change when I returned back to San Diego, I may not have a great opportunity awaiting my return. While I was nervous about choosing, I was steadfast that a decision had to be made. It took everything from me, knowing I was not going to be working this new program, but nonetheless, I made the difficult decision. And you can too. Know that. Believe in yourself, because as hard as anything is, don't let your music die within you. Do what's in your heart. When making tough choices, follow the melody that comes from your soul. It will steer the way.

So I went to London and had an amazing time. It was the trip of a lifetime. The workdays were intense but enjoyable, and I got the chance to work with many of the same people who were on the engineering team from the last project.

I did what I believed to be right even though there may have been adverse consequences. It was a very difficult personal decision because of my love for my job at the time. However, I knew I had to seize the opportunity to travel and work in a different part of the world. Two days after I made the decision, the program manager of the new program told me they decided to keep the position open for my return. Thankfully, it all worked out. If I had decided to stay in the States, or even hesitated in making a decision, I may have lost out on the chance to travel to London.

The same should be true to you and your life. We all face tough decisions, but when it comes down to it, the worst action is inaction. Think it through, follow your heart, and decide, decide, decide.

Facing the Fear and Doing it Anyway

We could have all of the best plans, biggest goals and crystal clear vision but without action, it is just not going to happen. It is incredibly easy to become completely overwhelmed and overcome by fear. Doubts can creep in, and you may say, "How am I ever going to do any of this?" Negative self-talk may rear its ugly head. To understand where this fear of decisions and decision-making comes from, we all have to look deep inside our beings to understand why a particular decision causes such anguish, grief, and stress.

I asked myself the same questions, and it all comes down to two simple things--self-doubt and consequences. When making difficult decisions, it is only natural to have personal doubt in your ultimate choice. The question we often ask ourselves is: What if I am wrong? Another fear that often presents itself is the fear of consequences. The question here that we often ask ourselves is: If I am wrong, how will that affect my life? Self-doubt and the fear of consequences are completely normal human responses. The key is how we choose to handle these physiological issues.

First and foremost, you have to acknowledge your self-doubt. Even give it a name. "Hey, Sam the self-doubt, I see you've come near." When challenging areas show up in your life, try to make a game out of it. Feel the fear, and do it anyway. Bingo! It is behind you. We have work to do. When I feel self-doubt with my decisions, I try to analyze where that self-doubt is coming from. Is it from a past bad experience? Is it because I am unclear of my decision to begin with? Is it because of others telling me it is a bad decision? All of these questions can lead to answers and clarity surrounding your self-doubt. These feelings should be expected with any decision, but the way you react and examine this emotion will be what helps you move through it and learn to handle it for the next time.

Furthermore, many people have significant fear of the consequences from their decisions. When I decided to go to London, I knew that there was a chance I could return with no job. Obviously that would be a terrible consequence to my actions and decision, but it was one I was willing to face. When we consider consequences, it is imperative to understand the value that should be given to your consequences. Some consequences are big and some are not. But if you take time to truly map out what your decisions may inevitably lead to, it will become much easier to not only appreciate your potential consequences, but also give them the appropriate attention that they deserve.

Self-doubt and consequences are certainly two fears that deserve your time and attention. But handling them in a proactive manner will surely alleviate much of the stress that they create and allow you to not become a victim of the paralysis they can often cause. You are strong enough to handle these fears and evaluate the situation to ensure you make a decision with a sound mind and a clear heart.

"Whatever you can do or dream you can, begin it.
Boldness has genius, power and magic in it."

—JOHANN WOLFGANG VON GOETHE

Take the Action, Let Go of the Result

Too often in life, we get so completely caught up in the result of what is going to happen that our focus gets completely out of whack. The result does not always justify the decision. More times than not, making the decision can be even more difficult than dealing with the results, even if they may not be positive ones. When imagineering your ideal life, you should anticipate making many difficult decisions. With every action, there will almost certainly be a reaction. These reactions can be both good and bad, but you have to remember that regardless, these reactions are not only natural, but also expected.

Of course, it is important to be very clear and specific on the results that you do want. By figuring that out first, you are on your way. But sometimes it's helpful to just move forward and adjust along the way if you see that your path is sending you in the wrong direction. You can't always control every outcome. Once you know and believe this, your path will become easier to travel.

When the negative thoughts I call the 'what-ifs' start coming up, all you have to do is I·G·N·O·R·E them, even if you have to start singing the letters out loud. 'What-ifs' are a waste of your precious time. That's right, precious time, because time is just that and you have to start being selective of how you choose to spend your time. In life, we only have a limited amount of time to spend reacting to specific experiences and occurrences.

Spending your attention on the results of your action can, at times, be unhealthy. Life will not always go as you may plan, and when it does not, reacting in a detrimental way only compounds the underlying problem. Always remember, the action is essential, the result is unpredictable. But whatever it may be, give yourself credit for acting, and don't spend so much time harping over the result.

The fact is, we all only have so much time, and you want to be able to look back and know you were the very best you could have been.

California Wildfires

During the 2007 wildfires in southern California, I was evacuated from my home, along with many neighbors, friends, and my sister's family. We all thankfully stayed safely at a friend's home with all our treasured belongings, the ones we could quickly pack in our cars. Amid the horrible dark red sky, the roar of the wind, the smoke and hard dust air, the sound of fire engines, it was absolutely terrifying. Fear crackled in the air.

We all got out safely, but the unknowns were the white elephant in the room. My precious little seven-year old nephew looked up to me with his big brown eyes and asked me, "Auntie, what if your house burns down?" with such a caring and soft voice.

I sat down, placed his hand in mine and said to him with his big worried eyes, "Dylan, the most important thing is that we are safe and here together; and whatever happens, we will handle it. Let's not worry ourselves with what-ifs. Now let's go play a game." And that was the end of that.

Just like that, we were focused on something more pleasant and in the moment. Thankfully neither of our homes were harmed, but the most important lesson here is that my nephew and I could have gone down that maniacal spiral of the 'what-if's' if I had not stopped it right then and there.

There will be many emotionally filled "what-if's" moments in your life. The significant piece to the puzzle is not the "what if" but rather the "what if I didn't." Be proud of yourself for action, rather than punishing yourself for the result. When we evacuated our houses, we knew deep down there was a chance we may never see them again. But by evacuating, we almost surely saved our lives. It would have been easy to regret that decision if we lost all of our belongings. We could have thought we should have stayed longer, filled our cars with more precious belongings, or taken out more insurance before this terrible act occurred. But rather, we all spent our time together, being thankful we were safe, and celebrating the fact that we acted quickly and were together.

So please, once you know the results you want to ultimately achieve, go for it. Take the actions necessary, and one day that result will come to fruition. Do not hesitate, show no regret, and do not spend endless precious moments beating yourself up if the 'what if's' become a reality.

Because no matter what, the "what if's" will always be worse than the "what if I did not's."

> *"If people only knew how hard I work to gain my mastery, it wouldn't seem so wonderful at all."*
>
> —Michelangelo

Action Analysis

As you move through your life, Imagineering an ideal timeline and putting it into effect, it is crucial to remember that you should always analyze your actions with a careful eye. Assessing your decisions is critical to your personal growth. Have you ever woken up feeling like you cannot endure another day of your current situation? Do you feel as if you are somehow just going through the motions? Deep in your gut, do you know there is something more out there for you?

So where are you? Are you right where you want to be? Are you questioning where you are and how you got here? It is interesting to look at life with this perspective because sometimes we just lose our place, and get caught in a funk. Self-reflection is a useful way to evaluate your actions and decisions and at times, provide positive feedback that can help you grow. I have found that asking good questions helps clarify what's going on inside of us.

It is easy to become complacent and forget to act. But it is even easier to act without reason and purpose. To make a decision, but never look back and decide if you could have made a better decision. Now I am not saying that you should have regret or punish yourself if you make a poor decision. Not at all. What I am saying is that you just reflect and scrutinize. Only then will you hold yourself accountable and ensure you stay the course.

If you do not take inventory of your life and truly acknowledge how you feel and acted, those feelings will show up in many different ways. Bottom line, you must face how you feel. When reviewing your decisions and action, take a look at these three vital considerations:

➢ **Face it.** See the situation for what it is regardless of emotion.

➢ **Feel it.** Now open up to how you truly feel about what you are facing.

➢ **Figure it out.** Once you have a handle on the situation and your feelings about it, you can then figure out your course of action in dealing with whatever challenges may come your way.

The idea of self-reflection comes from the sincere recognition of not being happy in the place you are right now. You may feel as if you are stuck. The best reason to get out of that place is because you cannot stand being in it anymore. That is what I mean by leverage. Basically, you have no choice but to move forward or move out because you can't stand your current situation another day.

Sometimes that feeling is just what we need to move, get going, and thinking differently. In these moments, staying in the same spot is much more painful than moving on. This feeling of somehow being stuck is good; it gets you moving and changing your direction. When life becomes too uncomfortable, this type of leverage is what helps get you out of your comfort zone. It is when you start making positive changes in your life and you start seeing yourself moving in the right direction.

"If you're going to attempt something new, don't try it. Do it, go full out. If you're going to make a mistake make a big one. Good entertainers do that all the time."

—CAROL BURNETT

Always Believe in Your Dreams

As you begin to make decisions and put your timeline into an active game plan, it is critical to your success that you constantly evaluate all parts of your life and each of the choices you make. When you are starting to take action on your dreams and goals, be careful with whom you share your story. When actions go wrong, it can be for many different reasons. You have control over many of those reasons. One of those choices you make as you travel through life, is who you surround yourself with throughout your journey.

I remember my good friend, an engineer, and I went out to lunch. I was telling him how I had decided to write a book. I told him that I had developed a concept and wanted to write a book *on how to architect our own lives.* I invited my friend to join me in writing the book. I shared with him that I was inspired to write because I had just returned from a fantastic one-week success workshop taught by Jack Canfield who co-wrote *Chicken Soup for the Soul.*

My engineer friend, like so many people who work in disciplines where answers are black and white, began to make fun of this kind of seminar and lightheartedly mocked my enthusiasm. He started to say, "Oh yeah, that is all the fluff stuff." Despite his misgivings, I rambled on and on enthusiastically about the seminar while he periodically inserted his joking derision. By the end of lunch as we were finishing, I said, "You know Chicken *Poop* for the Soul was a…"

I was going to say international bestseller but I stopped dead in my tracks. Had I actually just said the word "Poop!?" We both cracked up. I could not believe that all of his good-natured bantering had so quickly influenced me that I subconsciously called this insightful book "Chicken Poop" instead of "Chicken Soup."

The point here isn't about my wonderful friend's misgivings. But rather, it demonstrates that our actions are often times dictated by the people around us. Surround yourself with positive people and they will help guide you toward positive decisions. Encase your life with negativity and you too may make unfortunate mistakes, like I did above. Do not let someone else's thinking alter your STRONG positive feelings about life. Always believe in your dreams and be careful with whom you share them.

Little Bottles of Shampoo

When you take action, practice giving back. There are numerous charities to donate your time or money to. You will find that in life, you get when you give. What are you most passionate about? Is it children? Is it women in need? Is it the homeless? There are so many charities to be part of and a chance to give back.

Taking action and deciding to get involved in charities is extremely rewarding. For years, I had been receiving envelopes in the mail from the San Diego Rescue Mission. Finally, I decided to go down to see what it looked like and how I could help. I had been sending money at holiday times but I also thought about donating my time. I was nervous of feeling too upset in such a dire environment, but I mustered my courage to take a tour of the facility.

I saw the area of the shelter where thirty women stay each night, to avoid their abusive home situations. It was terrible. There were sleeping bags pushed together in this small space on the cold hard floor. I asked the shelter volunteer after seeing the facility what I could do to help. He mentioned they were in need of little bottles of shampoo, soaps, toothbrushes and toothpaste. I instantly had an idea.

I collected those little bottles from the hotels when I travel and since there are so many travelers at my work, I knew they collected them too. So, I started this charity drive every August at my work to collect all types of toiletries, regardless if they were from travel. The outpouring of support was incredible.

We ended up with boxes and boxes of little and big bottles of shampoo, conditioner, and other select toiletries. When I arrived at the mission, they were incredibly grateful and ecstatic for the generous donation. While it was a small amount of time on my part, it made a humungous difference in the lives of so many women at that shelter. I will always remember that first time I drove down to the mission, my entire car smelling of soap from all the boxes and boxes filled with these basic necessities the mission needed. I was so happy. I learned then and there taking just a little bit of action and following through is key.

Action is a powerful tool. You can truly change lives with action. It did not take a lot of effort to collect toothpaste and shampoo and drop it off at the mission. A few hours of work a week can help and inspire. When it comes down to it, giving to others is the most amazing action that you can take. Find your inspiration and a cause that resonates in your heart, and act quickly to make a difference, because the payback will be enormous.

The Power of Three

When it comes down to action and decision-making, your options are endless. Throughout my journey, I work hard to streamline my actions and keep them focused. I do this through the power of three. So many amazing things come in trios: The *Three Wise Men*, *Holy Trinity (Father, Son, Holy Spirit)*, "*Duty, Honor, Country*" and "*Body, Mind, Soul*" to give just a few examples. As I move through life, I try to breakdown each task I have into three's to help me manage different action steps and goals I want to take.

The same can be true to you. By breaking actions or decisions down to a set of three, you allow yourself the opportunity to concentrate on decisions and ensure they are the focal points of your thought process. Each day, write down three action steps you need to take to achieve your top three priorities. Then, each week, write down three goals you want to achieve that week. Breaking it down this way has made my days more focused, on-purpose and my life much more manageable. That is what I want for you.

Let's use the story of the *"Three Little Pigs"* to think about our own lives.

Like the homes of the three little piggies, do you want to build a life out of straw, out of wood, or out of brick? Do you want someone to come along one day to huff and puff your life down? How much effort are you going to put into creating your extraordinary life? What actions are you going to take to achieve your goals and get headed in the right direction?

Which little piggy are you? Are you the one that put in the effort to build the strong sturdy brick house? Or are you going to be like the other two little piggies' that did not put as much effort into building their homes. Think about it.

Go Forth And Act

Action is a powerful tool. The simple decision to move one foot in front of the other is an action we take everyday of our lives. And it has a compelling result. That is, when you act, you make a difference. You make a difference in your own life, in the lives of others, and in the world as a whole. Do not become overwhelmed by making difficult decisions, as doing so will inevitably lead to regret and remorse.

The focus of this chapter was on making decisions. When you act, remember that you have succeeded. Do not overvalue the result of your actions and understand that personal growth starts with putting the plan in motion. So many people do not put the plan in motion, but rather, sit on the sideline and watch life pass them by. Take pride in your ability to act and even if your actions do not work out exactly how you planned, pat yourself on the back for putting one foot in front of the other and achieving through acting.

Snippets: Architectural Achievement

The Longest Wall

The Great Wall of China is one of the greatest sites in the world. It stretches 5,500 miles (8,851km). It was originally designed to protect the northern borders of the Chinese Empire from invasion, an awe-inspiring feat of ancient architecture. This immense feat began construction in 5th century BC and continued through the 16th century. More than 20 dynasties were responsible for building the Great Wall.

The Great Roman Theater

The Roman Theater was the largest Coliseum ever built during the Roman Empire. The Coliseum could seat close to 50,000 spectators and was used for gladiatorial contests and public spectacles. Such events were of an enormous scale. The biggest recorded event is that of Trajan celebrating his victories in close to 107 contests involving 10,000 gladiators over the course of 123 days.

New York's Tallest Building

The New York Empire State Building was completed in 1931 at which time it was the world's tallest building. It held that record until 1972 when the World Trade Center was completed. The Empire State Building is 103 floors high, 1,454 ft high (443.2m) including the lightning rod. It also has an amazing 6,500 windows. Following the devastating destruction of the World Trade Towers on September, 11, 2001 the Empire State

Building again became New York City's tallest building.

Plus Up

➢ Are you ready to begin living that extraordinary life you have imagined?

➢ Have you set three goals to help you get closer to what you want to achieve?

➢ What simple consistent actions can you take each day to achieve them?

➢ Do you believe you can do it? (I believe in you!)

➢ How can you breakdown your actions into manageable and achievable components?

➢ Have you taken steps to finding the best mentors and coaches?

➢ Have you started surrounding yourself with like-minded individuals?

➢ Will you start living the life you want right now?

➢ Are you planning on taking action each day? How?

➢ Can you let go of the result and do it anyway?

➢ Are you willing to go back to the basics and the foundation of your dreams?

➢ Looking back on your life, what will be your legacy?

CONCLUSION

This book has presented numerous principles that you can implement into your life. We all have the opportunity to improve our lives and assess what we have achieved. Even the most accomplished people in the world can tweak and fine-tune their lives to ensure they are maximizing their potential in this world. Consider these concepts as you begin to grow and reach for all that life has to offer:

In Chapter 1,
"Why" *The Inspiration*
What is the inspiration for you and your extraordinary life? What makes your heart and spirit soar? What, when you do it, causes the world to fall away for you?

In Chapter 2,
"What" *The Vision*
What is your vision of your life? Be very specific and clear. What brings you the most happiness and peace?

In Chapter 3,
"How" *The Blueprint*
How are you going to start designing your life blueprint? How will you get from where you are to where you want to go?

In Chapter 4,
"Who" *The Architect*
You are the architect of your life. Who is that person and how will you be the master builder of the incredible life you were meant to lead?

In Chapter 5,
"Where" *The Site*
Keep Your Eye on Paradise. We discussed your environments and how they look. Where is this beautiful life of yours going to happen?

In Chapter 6,
"When" *The Timeline*
We all have to be realistic in how we choose to get from here to where we ultimately want to go. By breaking the milestones into manageable pieces it is possible to actually get to where you want to be. When do you envision that happening for you?

In Chapter 7,
"Action" *Now, Go Build It*
To achieve your vision you must take action. You must take a little action each day to achieve your vision. What are the actions you are going to start taking today to create a wonderful happy fulfilled life?

We have reached the conclusion of this book. I had envisioned the book long before I even began writing it. My education and background are in the fields of engineering, architecture, and computer science but my passion is living a life filled with happiness, peace, and joy, all while teaching others how to do the same.

You are very special. You were meant to leave your legacy, your fingerprint on this beautiful world. I believe in you. I truly want you to have a wonderful, happy love-filled life.

I have given you what I hope to be a practical tool belt to design a wonderful life filled with unlimited success. With these basic fundamentals, I know you can build and lead the extraordinary life you deserve and were meant to have. I believe that we all still have a child, a little girl or boy, inside of each of us. Be kind to that beautiful little kid.

By now, you should have a strong understanding about how to imagineer your ideal life. It all starts with finding your inspiration and figuring out exactly what motivates you to build your life. Next, like anything in life, you have to begin planning how you will create an extraordinary life. Considering what your vision is for the life you want to live is crucial at this point. We all have different goals and aspirations and to imagineer your perfect life, you have carve out a concrete vision.

Beginning to blueprint this vision is the next step on your journey. Before a beautiful home can be built, every aspect of it has to be considered, from the foundation to the frame, to the bricks, to the electricity and plumbing. If even one part of the blueprint is incorrect, the whole house may be affected. The same is true when building your ideal life. You have to put pen to paper and blueprint every detail that you hope will become a reality. This is the first step in implementing your vision.

Once you build your blueprint, it is time to begin making your vision a reality. You can plan for your entire life, but to reach your goals, you have to implement and act. Each day you have a responsibility to become a master builder and construct parts of your ideal life. Developing your design is the core facet to architecting and moving towards your life goals.

Once you have drafted your ideal blueprint, you will have to consider where you want to build your life. Finding an environment that resonates with your heart and soul is crucial to creating a happy and balanced lifestyle. As you imagineer the life you dream of, the journey will be a special one, filled with challenges and obstacles, but also victories and triumphs.

Only you can develop a supremely wonderful life of which you are proud. Creating this type of existence will allow you to make the most of each day you have on this earth and benefit both yourself and all of those that are lucky enough to be around you.

I wish you all the happiness in the world. God bless you and may all your dreams come true.

Acknowledgments

I would like to thank so many people for their encouragement and belief in me while writing this book:

To my dear Morgan James Publishing family; David Hancock, Rick Frishman, Margo Toulouse, Jim Howard, and Bethany Marshall for taking me under your wing and truly believing in me and my work. I feel blessed and honored to be part of the Morgan James family.

For the wonderful soul, Ken Blanchard, whose words inspired me to begin the journey of writing this book and doing me the honor of writing the Foreword for my very first book. I will be forever grateful to you for your fatherly kindness and incredible wisdom.

To my sister Dawn, my precious nephews Dylan and Grant, their father Tom, and cousins Eileen & Alan, for all your amazing encouragement, love, and support. Thank you for always believing in me.

To the exceptionally talented Justin Spizman for your friendship and being a critical key component in editing and working hard to finalize and make this manuscript a wonderful read. You have been an absolute Godsend. Thank you to his beautiful Mother, Robyn Spizman for recommending her remarkable son.

Enormous thanks to my wonderful friend Harry Smith, who helped me get through the first couple go-arounds of editing the manuscript. Harry inspired and encouraged me to pursue this journey.

I have tremendous gratitude for my dear friend and amazingly gifted Ann McIndoo, my author's coach, her wonderful assistant Mishael Patton, and Justin Sachs who helped me get this book out of my head and onto the page.

To my TUG (The Ultimate Game of Life) family; Jim Bunch, Doug Miller, Phil Black, Alexis Wagner, LuAnne Hage, and all the wonderful players, you truly inspired me and kept me going during this diligent process. I am so very grateful to you all.

For Karen Glass, former Disney editor extraordinaire, who diligently assisted me in the next few go-arounds of editing. I am so grateful we crossed paths.

Former Navy Lieutenant, John Mangan. Your mentoring about people, life, and excellence makes me treasure our friendship and thousands of walks.

My dear friend, Mike McCall, for his fatherly encouragement, insight and amazing wisdom. I will always cherish our talks, walks, and friendship.

For Dave & Doug Durham thank you for your wonderful friendship and brotherly love. I cherish you both.

To my dear friends: Debbie Abrams, Bruce Barbour (Jersey), Herman Bell, Terry Bitterlich & the Bitterlich clan, Craig & Diane Blatzheim, Mark Borowske, Diane Brockman, Alley Brown, Paul Cannon, Ed Carlevale, Mary Cessna, Jaime Coons, Craig & Natasha Duswalt, Marco Frazzini, David Garriott, Steven Hill, Arthur Samuel Joseph, Stephani Kassis-DiKiy, Derek Kennedy, Salahuddin Khan, Deb Krahling (for inviting Ken to the company), Juli Kramer, Mark Kramer, James Malinchak, Scott Mayer, Jim Miller, Barb Milligan, Nancy Mlynek, Garron Mobley, Jason Nast, Matt

& Inessa Neal, Jay O'Keefe, Noreen O'Mahoney, Daniel Ramirez, Cindy Reeves, Andre Richardson, Dianne Ricks, Sam Samson, Karla Scherer, Shari Smith, Michael Tardio, Jeffrey Wilson, Rosemary Wilson, Greg & Jen Van Ginkel, Pam & Mark Vriesenga, and Debra Zirolla, for all of you being incredibly supportive and encouraging during this whole big dream of mine. It is beyond words having such wonderful friends like you.

To my treasured childhood best friends: Pamela (Pnina) Dill, Dawn Marquez, Audrey Freiman, and Bob Kravitz for your everlasting friendship.

To my friend and confidante, Mary Ellen Bennett, for her incredible guidance, clarity on life, and depth of knowledge on human nature.

To Doc Schneider, for your mentoring, fun-loving attitude, and for believing in me from the very beginning.

Special love and thanks to one of my favorite teachers, Barbara DeAngelis. I am forever grateful for her amazing coaching, cheering me on, and truly believing in me.

An enormous thank you to my amazing coach, Jack Canfield for hours and hours of incredible teaching, wisdom, and insight.

Thank you world-class photographer and friend, Kevin Connors of Coast Highway Photo in Solana Beach, CA for shooting the cover in Del Mar, CA. You truly have a magical eye.

A very special thanks and warmest regards to Rachel Lopez my book designer. You have incredible talent and an amazing eye for detail.

To dearest Tamson Pechman who helped me get the 2nd edition of this book into tip-top shape. I am so grateful to she and her dear husband Bruce, who helped me get booked on my very first TV interview on "Good Morning San Diego."

ABOUT THE AUTHOR

Siobhan McKenna has worked in the Aerospace and Defense industry for over seventeen years as a software and systems engineer designing and developing large complex computer systems. Along with her education and experience in this technical arena, Siobhan has been studying and modeling successful people for twenty-five years.

She founded her company, "Mastery Builders," to help people define and live their ultimate lives. Siobhan has had a fascination with people who have been happy and ultimately live a wonderful and fulfilled life. This book is an accumulation of the wisdom and experience she has to share with you.

Author, speaker, life-coach, and engineer, Siobhan started her education studying Mechanical Engineering at Northeastern University in Boston, Massachusetts. She continued her education by earning her Bachelor's Degree from Arizona State University's Architecture School located in Tempe, Arizona. Siobhan also earned a Bachelors Degree in Computer Science from Coleman University in San Diego, California.

Using her knowledge of how complex systems are built and her passion for positive life creation, Siobhan's mission is to empower and inspire people around the world to design and build extraordinary lives.

BUY A SHARE OF THE FUTURE IN YOUR COMMUNITY

These certificates make great holiday, graduation and birthday gifts that can be personalized with the recipient's name. The cost of one S.H.A.R.E. or one square foot is $54.17. The personalized certificate is suitable for framing and will state the number of shares purchased and the amount of each share, as well as the recipient's name. The home that you participate in "building" will last for many years and will continue to grow in value.

Here is a sample SHARE certificate:

HABITAT FOR HUMANITY

THIS CERTIFIES THAT
YOUR NAME HERE
HAS INVESTED IN A HOME FOR A DESERVING FAMILY

1985-2005
TWENTY YEARS OF BUILDING FUTURES IN OUR
COMMUNITY ONE HOME AT A TIME

1200 SQUARE FOOT HOUSE @ $65,000 = $54.17 PER SQUARE FOOT
This certificate represents a tax deductible donation. It has no cash value.

YES, I WOULD LIKE TO HELP!

I support the work that Habitat for Humanity does and I want to be part of the excitement! As a donor, I will receive periodic updates on your construction activities but, more importantly, I know my gift will help a family in our community realize the dream of homeownership. **I would like to SHARE in your efforts against substandard housing in my community!** *(Please print below)*

PLEASE SEND ME _____ SHARES at $54.17 EACH = $ $_____

In Honor Of: _____

Occasion: (Circle One)   HOLIDAY   BIRTHDAY   ANNIVERSARY

     OTHER: _____

Address of Recipient: _____

Gift From: _____ *Donor Address:* _____

Donor Email: _____

I AM ENCLOSING A CHECK FOR $ $_____ PAYABLE TO HABITAT FOR HUMANITY **OR** PLEASE CHARGE MY VISA OR MASTERCARD *(CIRCLE ONE)*

Card Number _____ Expiration Date: _____

Name as it appears on Credit Card _____ Charge Amount $ _____

Signature _____

Billing Address _____

Telephone # Day _____ Eve _____

PLEASE NOTE: Your contribution is tax-deductible to the fullest extent allowed by law.
Habitat for Humanity • P.O. Box 1443 • Newport News, VA 23601 • 757-596-5553
www.HelpHabitatforHumanity.org

Printed in the USA
CPSIA information can be obtained
at www.ICGtesting.com
JSHW082347140824
68134JS00020B/1925

9 781614 481331